Published by Creative Education
123 South Broad Street, Mankato, Minnesota 56001

Creative Education is an imprint of The Creative Company.
Design by Stephanie Blumenthal
Production design by The Design Lab
Art direction by Rita Marshall

Photographs by Corbis (Niall Benvie, Bettmann, Sandy Felsenthal, Michael Freeman,
Farrell Grehan, Thomas A. Heinz, John Swope Collection, Catherine Karnow, Layne
Kennedy, Marvin Koner, Charles & Josette Lenars, Gail Mooney, Benjamin Rondel,
Bob Rowan; Progressive Image, G.E. Kidder Smith, Richard Hamilton Smith, Roger
Wood), Getty Images (Alfred Eisenstaedt/Time Life Pictures, Joe Munroe)

FRANK LLOYD

Writings of Frank Lloyd Wright are Copyright © 2005 The Frank Lloyd Wright
Foundation, Taliesin West, Scottsdale, AZ. Used with permission.

Library of Congress Cataloging-in-Publication Data

Fandel, Jennifer.
Frank Lloyd Wright / by Jennifer Fandel.
p. cm. — (Xtraordinary artists)
Includes index.
ISBN 1-58341-378-2
1. Wright, Frank Lloyd, 1867–1959—Juvenile literature. 2. Architects—United
States—Biography—Juvenile literature. I. Title. II. Series.

NA737.W7F285 2005
720'.92—dc22   2004063433

First edition

2 4 6 8 9 7 5 3 1

XTRAORDINARY ARTISTS

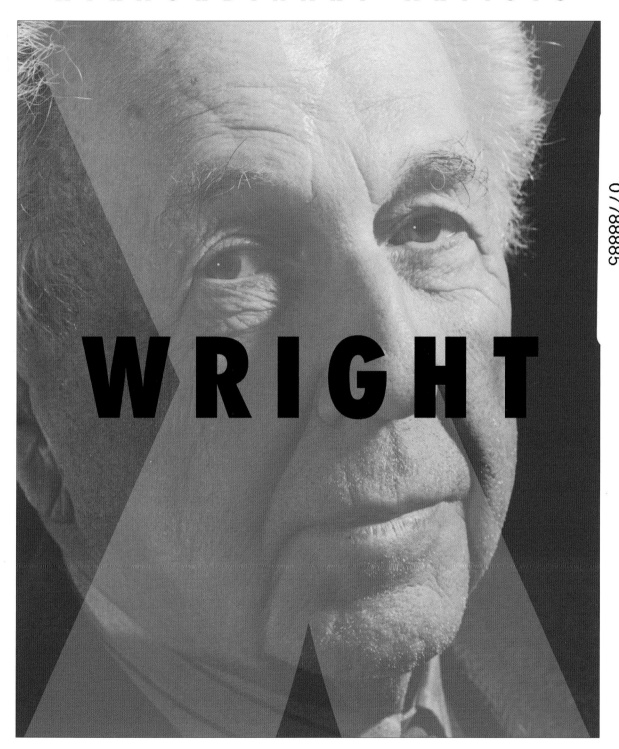

WRIGHT

JENNIFER FANDEL

CREATIVE EDUCATION

Throughout his life, Frank Lloyd Wright was fond of saying, "Early in life, I had to choose between honest arrogance and hypocritical humility. I chose honest arrogance and have seen no occasion to change." While the American architect's boastful nature and love of the spotlight helped him cultivate a legendary status, his buildings remain a true testimony to his genius. From foundation to ceiling, each structure captivates the imagination, embodying Wright's skillful union of modern materials and a nature-inspired design. Considered America's finest architect and one of the greatest 20th-century designers in the world, Frank Lloyd Wright looked beyond the building styles of the past and designed the future.

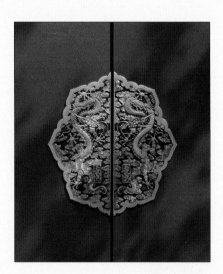

Frank Lloyd Wright was born on June 8, 1867, in Richland Center, Wisconsin, amidst rolling hills and fertile farmlands in the southern part of the state. His mother, Anna Lloyd Jones, was a teacher whose family had emigrated from Wales to Wisconsin in the 1840s. The Lloyd Joneses were a large, tight-knit, and prosperous family that valued education and held fast to their Welsh roots and Unitarian religious background.

Frank's father, William Wright, was a minister from the East Coast who had been educated in both medicine and law. A gifted musician and charming speaker, William easily drew attention to himself. His amiable personality opened doors for him, and he was constantly offered new jobs—as a pastor, lecturer, musician, and lawyer. In his restlessness, he moved his family with each opportunity that came along.

Wright's Wisconsin home, Taliesin, has been described by some as his autobiography embodied in wood and stone

The influence of both nature and geometry can be seen in much of Wright's work, including the triangular-shaped pool at Taliesin West

Frank was the oldest of Anna and William's three children, and Anna claimed to have foreseen her son's career in architecture before he was born. Destiny was a reoccurring theme in the Welsh legends that Anna's family cherished, and it played an important part in how she saw the world. To help Frank toward his "calling," Anna hung drawings of English chapels around his crib. Once he reached the age of seven, she introduced him to the Froebel method, a visual education technique involving wooden building blocks and colorful paper shapes. From this, Frank learned to see geometry and forms in nature—from the complex root system in trees to the pattern of petals on a flower.

A lifelong fascination with the shapes of nature provided Wright with ample sources of inspiration as he designed his now-famous buildings

7

"His intimacy with nature enabled him to translate it into architectural terms. In the patterns of nature, the formation of a snowflake . . . the indentations and lines in a jagged rock hanging over the sea, it was an inner beat, an inner rhythm he listened to . . . bringing never-ending variety into architecture."

— *Olgivanna Wright, Frank's third wife*

Even the Midway Barns at Wright's Taliesin estate in rural Wisconsin reflect his belief that buildings must grow naturally from their surroundings

Throughout Frank's childhood, his family moved around the East and Midwest. By the time they settled down in Wisconsin's capital city of Madison, 11-year-old Frank had lived in six different towns across four states. A shy boy, Frank enjoyed reading novels, playing the piano and viola, and painting. Preferring his own private world to interaction with his family or fellow classmates, Frank found sanctuary in his bedroom as a teenager. The warnings "Sanctum Sanctorum" (Latin for "Sacred Sanctuary") and "Keep Out" graced a sign outside his bedroom door. Inside the bedroom, nature scenes that he had painted decorated the walls.

While Frank's mother nurtured her son's artistic inclinations and held fast to her early visions of his architect future, she worried about his behavior as he grew older. When he did leave the security of his bedroom, he seemed intent to dress and act the part of a fashionable dandy—wearing such showy items as a stovepipe hat—instead of presenting himself as a young man of substance. He had difficulty fitting in among his peers, as he rarely dropped the romantic guises he had dreamed up for himself.

Hoping to toughen him up and shake him from his dreamy tendencies, Frank's parents sent him to work each summer on his uncle James Lloyd Jones's farm in Spring

Although he did not enjoy the work, summers on his uncle's farm in Wisconsin gave Wright the opportunity to experience the natural world

Green, a rural town a short distance from Madison. The farm's physical labor and grueling schedule, which included rising at 4:00 A.M. to milk cows, was completely foreign to Frank. Accustomed to the comforts of town life, the teenager was also shocked by the constant amount of work required to run a farm, from tending livestock to chopping firewood and harvesting crops. He despised the work and even tried running away on more than one occasion.

Despite his dislike for farm work, Frank fell in love with the land that surrounded him. Steep hillsides were broken by jagged limestone outcroppings, and the Wisconsin River curved through the valley below. Even when he ran away from the farm, he never

went far, finding a comfortable hay bale on which to rest or discovering a new bluff from which to sit and think.

Surrounded by his stalwart uncle and cousins, Frank was left little opportunity for idle dreaming, however. Whenever he was caught slacking, Uncle James recited his favorite adage, "Add tired to tired, and then add it again." The teenager grew annoyed hearing it repeated so often, but it made a lasting impression on him. As an adult, Frank would reflect happily on the phrase and on those summers on the farm. No matter how enormous the task or how daunting the obstacle he faced, the adage reminded Frank that a strong will and hard work could take him to a better future.

In 1885, before he turned 18, Frank suddenly found himself on his own. His parents divorced, and he would never again see his father. Quitting his last year of high school, Frank found work as a junior draftsman for a civil engineer at the University of Wisconsin in Madison and enrolled for two semesters of college courses there. Frank's mother expected him to take his father's place and support the family, but Frank hated to be practical with his money. He spent most of his paychecks on extravagant clothes, books, and trips to the theater—anything to show that he was a man of possibility, class, and style.

While at the university, Frank got his first taste of architectural design work. His uncle Jenkin Lloyd Jones had commissioned Chicago architect Joseph Lyman Silsbee to design a chapel near Spring Green, and Frank was allowed to assist in the interior design, becoming known in family circles as "the boy architect." In 1887, Frank moved to Chicago, taking a draftsman's position at Silsbee's firm. That year, Frank's schoolteacher aunts asked him to design a building for their school, Hillside, near Spring Green. This was his first building design to be executed, and Frank suddenly saw his future. He began signing his drawings "Frank Lloyd Wright, Architect." After only one year under Silsbee, Frank was hired at Adler and Sullivan, one of Chicago's most prestigious and cutting-edge architectural firms.

The 10-story Wainwright Building in St. Louis, Missouri, built in 1891 by Adler and Sullivan, was one of the first skyscrapers in the world

Oak Park, Illinois, boasts many buildings designed by Wright, including his first home, which he built with $5,000 borrowed from Louis Sullivan

In 1889, Frank married Catherine Tobin, an intelligent and spirited woman from a well-to-do Unitarian family. Frank was 22, and Catherine was 18. Already in Louis Sullivan's good favor, Frank asked him for a loan to build a home in Oak Park, a developing suburb of Chicago. In 1890, the first of Frank and Catherine's six children was born.

Sullivan immediately recognized Frank's immense talent; by the age of 22, Frank was the company's chief designer and was supervising 30 draftsmen. Wealthy clients occasionally approached the firm with requests for residential designs. These projects were an inconvenience to Sullivan, who preferred high-profit commercial designs, but they were the jobs Frank wanted. As his reputation for residential design spread, Frank began moonlighting after hours, designing houses around Chicago and its suburbs. This was against the firm's policy, and when confronted about his work after hours, Frank quit, confident of making his own opportunities.

Thinking of windows as parts of—rather than holes in—the wall, Wright often included geometrically patterned stained glass in his buildings

15

"Some of these [houses] seem to grow out of the ground as naturally as the trees, and to express our hospitable suburban American life, a life of indoors and outdoors, as spontaneously as certain Italian villas express the more pompous and splendid life of those old gorgeous centuries."

—— *American writer Harriet Monroe, commenting on Wright's work at a 1907 exhibition*

Built in 1902, the Fred B. Jones house is one of seven Wright-designed Prairie Style homes on Lake Delavan in Wisconsin

In 1893, when he was 26, Frank went into private practice. He developed what he called Prairie Style homes—stone and wood homes with an open floor plan, a center fireplace, and walls of endless windows to let in natural light. For Frank, this wasn't a passing style, but the groundwork for his theory of organic architecture. His concept had its roots in Louis Sullivan's theory of "Form Follows Function." Before Sullivan, architects thought little of a building's practical use and simply reused the styles of past ages. Sullivan had helped launch architecture into the modern era by proposing that the design of a building impact its purpose. But Frank took Sullivan's theory a step farther, insisting on a design employing absolute harmony between the land, the materials, the building's function, and its occupants. He expressed this theory with the phrase "Form and Function Are One."

In his first year of private practice, Frank received five commissions, or orders, for

residential designs. For the next seven years, he had beyond steady work, with up to nine commissions a year. An excellent self-promoter, he published articles, gave speeches, and exhibited models and designs, including a solo exhibit in 1907 at the Art Institute of Chicago. Although many of his wealthy and often conservative clients thought his designs a bit too adventurous, Frank relied on the traits he had inherited from his father—charm, humor, and a way with words—to talk them into approving his plans.

The citizens of Chicago soon came to recognize the man with the broad-brimmed hat whose hair grew slightly over his collar. Frank often wore a dramatic cape and carried a cane, which he used to gesture grandly and accentuate the importance of his ideas. From 1900 on, his name would be a constant feature in the newspapers. And publicity, good or bad, was something that Frank never seemed to mind.

Between 1894 and 1911, Frank designed 135 buildings throughout the United States, focusing most of his efforts on residential design. Yet in spite of his success, he grew unhappy toward the end of this period. Not yet 40 years old, Frank felt restless: he found domestic life in Oak Park oppressive, and his work no longer held the spark of his earlier years. To escape his dissatisfaction, he abandoned his family and traveled to Europe with Mamah Cheney, the wife of a client. From 1909 to 1910, Frank lived in Berlin, Germany, and Florence, Italy, while working on the first foreign publication of his designs.

When he returned to Oak Park, Frank's residential design opportunities had largely vanished. Most of his clients found his behavior deplorable, and the newspapers' cov-

erage of the scandal had marred his reputation far beyond Chicago. It was then, having recently inherited land in Spring Green, that Frank began building his artistic retreat and eventual home, Taliesin. In 1911, when Frank and Mamah moved into Taliesin, the gossip about their lives still hadn't subsided. Frank explained himself by saying, "The ordinary man cannot live without rules to guide his conduct. It is infinitely more difficult to live without rules, but that is what the really honest, sincere, thinking man is compelled to do."

Around this time, Frank received a number of commissions for commercial structures. One of his most striking designs was a beer garden, restaurant, and dance

The heart of Taliesin was Wright's personal design studio, where he must have spent countless hours perfecting his creations

19

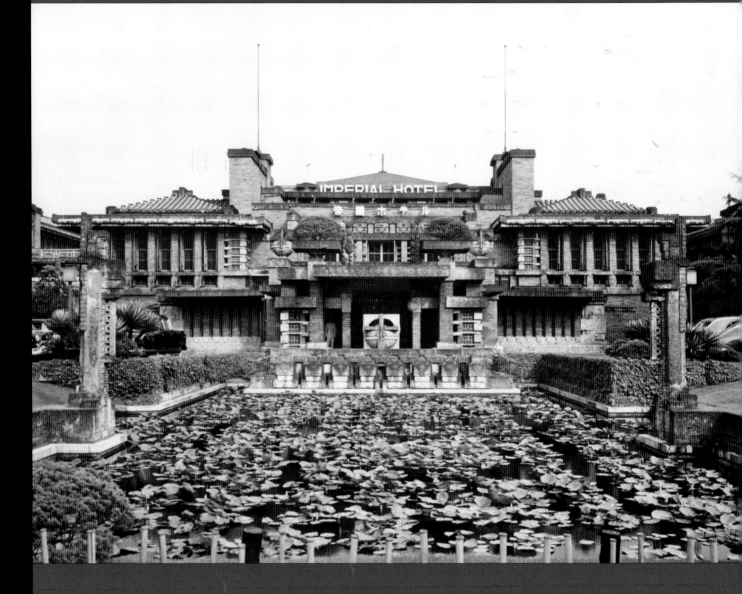

hall complex in Chicago called Midway Gardens. In 1914, while he was working on the project, tragedy struck at Taliesin. A crazed servant killed Mamah, her two children, and four visitors and set fire to the home. Some viewed the event as punishment for Frank's immoral behavior, and many wondered if the misfortune would spell the end of his career. Despite Frank's immense sorrow, quitting was not an option to him. The only part of his home that survived the fire was his studio, and Frank took it as a sign: he would rebuild Taliesin and continue his work.

Nearly two years later, in 1916, Frank gained a foothold in international design with his $4.5-million commission for the new Imperial Hotel in Tokyo, Japan. After

"Mr. Wright was a 'practical visionary.' He could talk about architectural ideas and about pouring a concrete wall and make all of it sound equally real and equally important. He loved the luxuries, but also as a kind of balance he appreciated the hardships, welcomed a chance to overcome them."

— *John Rattenbury, a Taliesin Fellowship apprentice*

experiencing an earthquake in Japan, he designed the building in flexible sections that could expand and contract in a tremor. In 1923, a year after the Imperial Hotel was completed, one of the largest earthquakes of the 20th century struck Tokyo. Not only did the structure hold up with only slight damage, but it was so structurally safe that it became a shelter for earthquake refugees.

During the six years it took to build the hotel, Frank spent most of his time in Japan, a country whose design principles of simplicity and harmony with nature appealed to him immensely. During these years, he found companionship with an American woman named Miriam Noel. Their relationship was a rocky one that lasted nine years. In 1923, they married, but Miriam left him after only six months.

In late 1924, Frank met Olgivanna Lazovich Hinzenberg, a young Montenegrin dancer and intellectual, at a ballet performance in Chicago. She was 26, and he was 57. They immediately fell in love and had a baby, a daughter named Iovanna, in late 1925. In all of his relationships, Frank's personality traits—his self-centeredness, mercurialness, and obsession with work—had made life difficult for spouses and companions. Although he changed little, Frank found a matching artistic spirit and a selfless companion in Olgivanna. They were married in 1928.

In the late 1920s and early '30s, the Great Depression froze most design projects in America. To insure a steady income for his family, Frank wrote and lectured around the world

on his design philosophies. He and Olgivanna also began a fellowship program at Taliesin. Through the program, talented young architects would learn the art of organic architecture through design work and labor on the Wrights' self-sustaining farm. Frank's reputation attracted immediate recruits, and the Taliesin Fellowship quickly became famous internationally.

With his new team of fellowship assistants ("the fingers of my hand," as Frank referred to them), Frank was able to take on more design work, and he came out of the depression with ideas enough to redesign the world. In interviews and casual conversations, when asked to name his masterpiece, Frank always replied, "The next one." In the beginning of 1943, he had no idea how true his words would turn out to be.

On October 21, 1959, upper 5th Avenue in Manhattan was buzzing with activity. Men in sharp suits and women in fitted dresses spilled down the block, waiting to enter Frank Lloyd Wright's crowning achievement, a museum of modern and contemporary art called the Solomon R. Guggenheim Museum. Referred to by Frank as an "inverted ziggarat," the curved white structure was unlike any building the crowd had ever seen.

The wonder of that day had actually been set in motion 16 years earlier, when Frank received his commission for the project in a letter from the museum's curator, Hilla Rebay. In that 1943 letter, she told him of her grandiose expectations for the project, exclaiming,

"I need a fighter, a lover of space, an agitator, a tester and a wise man. . . . I want a temple of spirit, a monument!" Frank knew he was the man to deliver such a building.

Despite Frank's enthusiasm, the project took more than a decade and a half. In the summer of 1943, Frank and the project's benefactor, Solomon R. Guggenheim, a multimillionaire who made his fortune in mining, signed the design contracts. In a letter to Rebay, Frank expressed how urgent the project was to him. He wrote, "I am so full of ideas for our museum that I am likely to blow up or commit suicide unless I can let them out on paper." In 1944, once the building site was selected, Frank began the process of drawing and revising his ideas, making more than 100 sketches.

With the museum, Wright broke up the rectangular-shaped grid precedent in New York, a city he considered overbuilt and overpopulated

In 1946, Frank revealed his vision of the building with a cutaway model of its exterior and interior. Over the next 10 years, he confronted skeptical city commissioners in an effort to get a building permit for his innovative structure. In the end, Frank told his Taliesin apprentices, he designed the building to please no one but himself. In 1956, groundbreaking ceremonies took place, and the building finally began.

Starting in August 1956, New Yorkers watched with curiosity and awe as an odd-shaped structure grew out of molded concrete and reinforced steel from the plot of cleared land. Among the boxy, monotone high-rises of 5th Avenue across from Central

Emphasizing natural elements in the Guggenheim Museum's design, Wright created a skylight and used earthy colors such as beige and brown.

Park, the Guggenheim Museum emerged as an eye-catching white building that broke up the skyline with its sweeping curves and inverted cone design.

Even more striking than the exterior was the marriage of form and function inside the building. Most previous museums were designed in square grids that required their patrons to cross through previously seen exhibit halls in order to enter another wing. Frank was sure he could avoid this traditional, and often tiresome, design. Carrying the curves of the outside structure to the inside of the building, he

designed a gradual ramp that led patrons from exhibit to exhibit seamlessly after riding an elevator to the top. It was as if one floor flowed into the next. From any position on the ramp, viewers could see the evolution of an artist's career, and, looking toward the building's center, they could see the museum's collection as a whole. In addition, Frank incorporated natural lighting with a large circular skylight and lowered the ceiling height to create a greater sense of intimacy with the art and the museum space.

As was common of Frank's work, his radical design drew considerable fire from critics. When artists complained that his building would overshadow the art housed in the museum, Frank wrote, "On the contrary, [the museum was designed] to make the building and the painting an uninterrupted, beautiful symphony such as never existed in the World of Art before."

While touring the museum on its opening day, the nearly 3,000 patrons remarked little on the works by Wassily Kandinsky, Marc Chagall, Paul Klee, and Pablo Picasso.

"The only real figure in the world of the arts that equaled him in the twentieth century, I think, was Picasso. Another figure with its roots, with its legs planted in the nineteenth century but the body did this great jump into the twentieth century."

— *Paul Goldberger, architecture critic and writer for* The New Yorker

Instead, they focused on the spaces they were walking through, taking in the breathtaking white curves. Olgivanna affectionately termed the museum Frank's "Miracle on 5th Avenue," and those words seemed fitting for that October day. Most of the patrons—art aficionados, architecture buffs, and curious citizens alike—had only read about the experience of Frank Lloyd Wright's modern designs, and they were dazzled by what they saw. In their eyes, the Guggenheim was not just a building; it was a marvel—a masterpiece—that rose from the street.

Shattering existing ideas of what a museum should be, the Guggenheim has attracted millions of visitors to its multileveled exhibit space

31

"Part of his greatness was the degree to which he was in touch with American life, American psychology and to some extent, the degree to which he was in touch with the 20th century. . . . He understood the car. He understood the modern workplace."

— *American architect Robert A.M. Stern*

In 1930, at an age when many of his colleagues were contemplating the ease of retirement, 63-year-old Frank hit a new stride, producing some of the most creative and noteworthy designs of his career. In the realm of residential design was Frank's 1935 masterpiece Fallingwater, built in Pennsylvania for Edgar J. Kaufmann, Sr., a wealthy Pittsburgh department store owner. Kaufmann's family wanted a home with views of their favorite waterfall. Frank responded by anchoring the house's foundation into the waterfall's rock ledges, creating a structure that was one with the nature that surrounded it.

A year later, Frank designed a stunning commercial structure, the S.C. Johnson and Son Administration Building in Racine, Wisconsin. Striving to infuse the American workplace with artistry and a connection to nature, Frank designed glass tube walkways and skylights that let an abundance of natural light into the building. The centerpiece of his design was an open workspace filled with lily pad-shaped columns made of steel-enforced concrete and covered with pyrex, a shiny, heat-resistant glass.

By 1937, Frank and his family—Olgivanna, their daughter Iovanna, and his adopted daughter Svetlana—were spending their winters at Taliesin West, a desert retreat near Scottsdale, Arizona. After Frank suffered a serious bout of pneumonia in 1936, his doctor had encouraged him to move to a milder climate during the winter months. The following

After viewing the waterfall, Wright wrote to Edgar Kaufmann that Fallingwater was taking shape in his mind "to the music of the stream"

year, 70-year-old Frank built Taliesin West, a stunning collection of buildings constructed of redwood and concrete mixed with bright desert stones.

Besides design commissions, Frank received many awards and honors in the last 30 years of his life. In 1949, at the age of 82, he was awarded the Gold Medal from the American Institute of Architecture, an award that the institute had bestowed on less talented architects in prior years. To make his simultaneous pleasure and displeasure

known, Frank began his acceptance speech by saying, "Well, it's about time." In addition to this major award, he received honorary doctorates from Princeton and the University of Wisconsin. Also, to commemorate his achievements on an annual basis, both Chicago and Spring Green began celebrating a "Frank Lloyd Wright Day."

In 1957, Frank received 40 commissions, a record for his career. The work was showing no sign of letting up, and neither was the 90-year-old architect. While he let his

Wright's influence can be seen in many works by other architects, including this church set among red rock formations near Sedona, Arizona

Taliesin assistants take on more of the drawing work, Frank was awake early every morning "playing" with his T-square, triangle, and compass, working out new designs. Between the ages of 75 and 91, he designed more than 500 projects—more than half of the design work that he produced throughout his seven-decade career. Of his total designs, he lived to see 532 structures completed.

Although Frank spent much of his later years working, he seldom turned down an interview or speaking engagement. In one national television interview, the notoriously outspoken architect boasted, "Having now had the experience [of building] 769 buildings, it's quite easy for me to shake them out of my sleeve. It's amazing what I could do for this

Wright's unique style extended not only to a building's exterior, but also to its interior spaces and furnishings, such as these Prairie Style chairs

"Mr. Wright was marvelous to work with. His sense of mission permeated his thinking and the drawings that he spread out before us—ever repeating that a better world will grow out of better creative solutions, better design. Each time he sat down at the drafting board, we sensed the power of his intent."

— *Edgar Tafel, a Taliesin Fellowship apprentice*

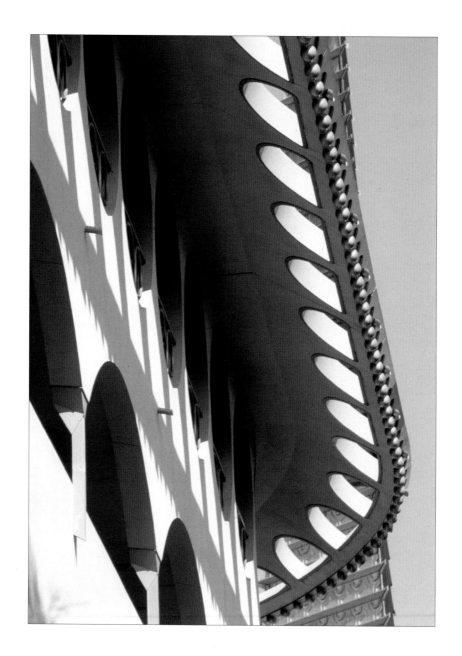

country." At other times, however, Frank became deeply reflective about his architectural legacy. In a speech toward the end of his life, he said, "I do not consider myself a success. I feel, rather, that I am a brilliant failure, because as yet the United States has no organic architecture."

Only months away from his 92nd birthday, Frank was energetic and in good health. Then, one night in early April 1959, he was rushed to the hospital with severe stomach pains. After a successful operation for an intestinal blockage, Frank looked to be on his way to a full recovery. But on April 9, in a hospital in Phoenix, Arizona, he quietly passed away.

Among his later works, Wright designed this concrete house in Phoenix, Arizona, for David Wright, his fourth child by his first wife

Almost 50 years after his death, Wright is still considered by many to be the greatest American architect of all time

Frank's Taliesin apprentices drove their teacher's body back to his beloved Wisconsin to be buried. On the day of the funeral, more than 200 mourners walked behind a horse and cart carrying Frank's flower-draped coffin. They walked through the lands that had nourished and inspired him, stopping at his resting place in the family graveyard. "Love of an idea is love of God" is all that his simple stone said.

"As a leader of revolt against dead custom Frank Wright has come into touch with the younger spirits because of his own youth and . . . because he has entered into every part of it with a zeal and courage which are a perpetual inspiration to those who understand and know him best."

— *Robert C. Spencer, Jr., a Prairie School architect and Wright colleague*

Frank Lloyd Wright was a prolific writer and lecturer on his theories and philosophy of architectural design. The following excerpts, taken from works published in 1909, 1914, and 1931, show the development of Wright's ideas on organic architecture, from his middle years to his later years as an elder architect speaking to his followers.

The following excerpt is from *Ausgefuhrte Bauten und Entwurfe von Frank Lloyd Wright* (*Completed Buildings and Designs by Frank Lloyd Wright*). Published in Berlin, Germany, in 1909, this was Wright's first book-length publication.

In America each man has a peculiar, inalienable right to live in his own house in his own way. He is a pioneer in every right sense of the word. His home environment may face forward, may portray his character, tastes, and ideas, if he has any, and every man here has some somewhere about him.

This is a condition at which Englishmen or Europeans, facing toward traditional forms which they are in duty bound to preserve, may well stand aghast. An American is in duty bound to establish traditions in harmony with his ideals, but still unspoiled sites, his industrial opportunities, and industrially he is more completely committed to the machine than any living man. It has given him the things which mean mastery over an uncivilized land—comfort and resources.

His machine, the tool in which his opportunity lies, can only murder the traditional forms of other peoples and earlier times. He must find new forms, new industrial ideals, or stultify both opportunity and forms. But underneath forms in all ages were certain conditions which determined them. In them all was a human spirit in accord with which they came to be; and where the forms were true forms, they will be found to be organic forms—an outgrowth, in other words, of conditions of life and work they arose to express. They are beautiful and significant, studied in this relation. They are dead to us, borrowed as they stand.

I have called this feeling for the organic character of form and treatment the Gothic spirit, for it was more completely realized in the forms of that architecture, perhaps, than any other. At least the infinitely varied forms of that architecture are more obviously and literally organic than any other, and the spirit in which they were conceived and wrought was one of absolute integrity of means to ends. In this spirit America will find the forms best suited to her opportunities, her aims, and her life.

All the great styles, approached from within, are spiritual treasure houses to architects. Transplanted as forms, they are tombs of a life that has been lived.

The following excerpt is from "Taliesin," an article published in *The Architectural Record* in May 1914. "Romeo and Juliet" in the article refers to a windmill that Wright designed.

Taliesin was the name of a Welsh Poet. A druid-bard or singer of songs who sang to Wales the glories of Fine Art. Literally the Welsh word means "shining brow." Many legends cling to the name in Wales.

This hill on which Taliesin now stands as "brow" was one of my favorite places when I was a boy, for pasque flowers grew there in March sun while snow still streaked the hillsides.

When you are on its crown you are out in mid-air as though swinging in a plane, as the Valley and two others drop away leaving the tree-tops all about you. "Romeo and Juliet" stands in plain view to the southeast, the Hillside Home School just over the ridge.

As "the boy" I had learned the ground-plan of the region in every line and feature.

Its "elevation" for me now is the modelling of the hills, the weaving and the fabric that clings to them, the look of it all in tender green or covered with snow or in full glow of summer that bursts into the glorious blaze of autumn.

I still feel myself as much a part of it as the trees and birds and bees, and red barns, or as the animals are, for that matter. . . .

Architecture, by now, was mine. It had come by actual experience to mean to me something out of the ground of what we call "America," something in league with the stones of the field, in sympathy with "the flower that fadeth, the grass that withereth," something of the prayerful consideration for the lilies of the field that was my gentle grandmother's. Something natural to the change that was "America" herself.

And it was unthinkable that any house should be put on that beloved hill.

I knew well by now that no house should ever be on any hill or on anything. It should be of the hill, belonging to it, so hill and house could live together each the happier for the other. That was the way everything found round about it was naturally managed, except when man did something. When he added his mite he became imitative and ugly. Why? Was there no natural house? I had proved, I felt, that there was, and now I, too, wanted a natural house to live in myself. I scanned the hills of the region where the rock came cropping out in strata to suggest buildings. How quiet and strong the rock-ledge masses looked with the dark red cedars and white birches, there, above the green slopes. They were all part of the countenance of southern Wisconsin.

I wished to be part of my beloved southern Wisconsin and not put my small part of it out of countenance. Architecture, after all, I have learned, or before all, I should say, is no less a weaving and a fabric than the trees. And as anyone might see, a beech tree is a beech tree. It isn't trying to be an oak. Nor is a pine trying to be a birch although each makes the other more beautiful when seen together.

The world has had appropriate buildings before—why not more appropriate buildings now than ever before? There must be some kind of house that would belong to that hill, as trees and the ledges of rock did; as Grandfather and Mother had belonged to it, in their sense of it all.

Yes, there must be a natural house, not natural as caves and log-cabins were natural but native in spirit and making, with all that architecture had meant whenever it was alive in times past. Nothing at all that I had ever seen would do. This country had changed all that into something else. Grandfather and Grandmother were something splendid in themselves that I couldn't imagine in any period houses I had ever seen. But there was a house that hill might marry and live happily with ever after. I fully intended to find it. I even saw, for myself, what it might be like and began to build it as the "brow" of the hill.

The following excerpt is from "To the Young Man in Architecture," which appeared in Wright's 1931 publication *Two Lectures in Architecture.*

Organic architecture seeks superior sense of use and a finer sense of comfort, expressed in organic simplicity. That is what you, young man, should call architecture. Use and comfort in order to become architecture must become spiritual satisfactions wherein the soul insures a more subtle use, achieves a more constant repose. So, architecture speaks as poetry to the soul. In this machine age to utter this poetry that is architecture, as in all other ages, you must learn the organic language of the natural which is ever the language of the new. To know any language you must know the alphabet. The alphabet in architecture in our machine age is the nature of steel, glass and concrete construction,—the nature of the machines used as tools, and the nature of the new materials to be used. . . .

Yes, modern architecture is young architecture,—the joy of youth must bring it. The love of youth, eternal youth must develop and keep it. You must see this architecture as wise, but not so much wise as sensible and wistful,—nor any more scientific than sentient, nor so much resembling a flying machine as a masterpiece of the imagination.

Oh yes, young man; consider well that a house is a machine in which to live, but by the same token a heart is a suction-pump. Sentient man begins where that concept of the heart ends.

Consider well that a house is a machine in which to live but architecture begins where that concept of the house ends. All life is machinery in a rudimentary sense, and yet machinery is the life of nothing. Machinery is machinery only because of life. It is better for you to proceed from the generals to the particulars. So do not rationalize from machinery to life. Why not think from life to machines? The utensil, the weapon, the automaton—all are appliances. The song, the masterpiece, the edifice are a warm outpouring of the heart of man,—human delight in life triumphant: we glimpse the infinite.

That glimpse or vision is what makes art a matter of inner experience,—therefore sacred, and no less but rather more individual in this age, I assure you, than ever before. . . .

Eye-weary of reiterated bald commonplaces wherein light is rejected from blank surfaces or fallen dismally into holes cut in them, organic architecture brings the man once more face to face with nature's play of shade and depth of shadow seeing fresh vistas of native creative human thought and native feeling presented to his imagination for consideration. This is modern.

The sense of interior space as reality in organic architecture coordinates with the enlarged means of modern materials. The building is now found in this sense of interior space; the enclosure is no longer found in terms of mere roof or walls but as "screened"—space. This reality is modern.

In true modern architecture, therefore, the sense of surface and mass disappears in light, or fabrications that combine it with strength. And this fabrication is no less the expression of principle as power-directed-toward-purpose than may be seen in any modern appliance or utensil machine. But modern architecture affirms the higher human sensibility of the sunlit space. Organic buildings are the strength and lightness of the spiders' spinning, buildings qualified by light, bred by native character to environment—married to the ground. That is modern!

1867

Frank Lloyd Wright is born in Richland Center, Wisconsin, on June 8.

1885

Wright leaves high school; he begins studying and working at the University of Wisconsin.

1887

Wright goes to work under architect Joseph Lyman Silsbee in Chicago.

1888

Wright begins a six-year stint under renowned architect Louis Sullivan at the Chicago architectural firm Adler and Sullivan.

1889

Wright marries Catherine Tobin and designs their Oak Park, Illinois, home.

1893

Wright opens his own firm in Chicago; five years later, he expands his Oak Park home and moves his practice there.

1900

Wright designs his first Prairie Style residence.

1909

Wright moves to Berlin, Germany, with Mamah Cheney; his first foreign collection of designs is published.

1911

Wright builds Taliesin on family land in Spring Green, Wisconsin, and Mamah moves there with him.

1914

A servant murders Mamah and burns Taliesin; Wright rebuilds the next year.

1916

Wright receives the Imperial Hotel commission in Tokyo, Japan, and soon moves to Japan.

1924

Wright meets Olgivanna Lazovich Hinzenberg, and they have a daughter named Iovanna the following year. They marry four years later.

1932

Wright opens Taliesin as an architectural fellowship.

1943

Wright receives his commission for the Solomon R. Guggenheim Museum in New York.

1949

Wright is awarded the Gold Medal from the American Institute of Architecture.

1959

Wright dies in Phoenix, Arizona, two months shy of his 92nd birthday.

Adler and Sullivan — *A Chicago design firm that gained prominence with its visually appealing skyscrapers and other commercial structures in the late 1800s and early 1900s*

cantilevered — *A term used to describe a long beam that is mounted to a structure at one end and left free at the other*

draftsman — *A person who assists an architect, drawing what the architect designs*

Great Depression — *A time in American history, lasting from 1929 to 1941, when the stock market crashed, businesses failed, and unemployment skyrocketed*

Joseph Lyman Silsbee — *A Chicago architect known for his homey and intricate residential designs for the wealthy in the late 1800s and early 1900s*

Louis Sullivan — *A late 19th- and early 20th-century American architect whose design principle of "form influences function" encouraged architects to create designs to complement a building's use*

open floor plan — *An interior design plan that uses columns instead of walls for ceiling support, allowing rooms to flow into one another*

organic architecture — *Wright's theory of harmony between all aspects of a building—from its residents and purpose to its materials and location*

Prairie Style — *Wright's early residential style, which maximized connections between nature and the Midwestern lifestyle; his followers were referred to as the Prairie School*

Unitarian — *A Christian religion that holds as its foundation a freedom from strict religious doctrine; instead, reason, conscientiousness, religious tolerance, and goodness are stressed*

ziggarat — *A pyramid-shaped tower that has steps leading to the top*

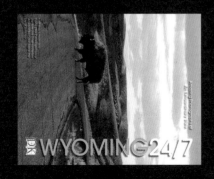

Put any picture you want on any state book cover. Makes a great gift. Go to www.america24-7.com/customcover

CORBIN

Harland Sanders's fried chicken recipe was so popular that Governor Ruby Laffoon named him a Kentucky Colonel in 1935. Kentucky governors have conferred the honorific title on many, including Bing Crosby and Pope John Paul II. The Colonel's original restaurant in Corbin is now a museum, just off Interstate '75.

Photo by Charles Bertram

Kentucky 24/7 is the sequel to *The New York Times* bestseller *America 24/7* shot by tens of thousands of digital photographers across America over the course of a single week. We would like to thank the following sponsors, the wonderful people of Kentucky, and the talented photojournalists who made this book possible.

DK

LONDON, NEW YORK, MUNICH, MELBOURNE, and DELHI

Created by Rick Smolan and David Elliot Cohen

24/7 Media, LLC
PO Box 1189
Sausalito, CA 94966-1189
www.america24-7.com

First Edition, 2004
04 05 06 07 08 10 9 8 7 6 5 4 3 2 1

Published in the United States by
DK Publishing, Inc.
375 Hudson Street
New York, NY 10014

DK Publishing, Inc. offers special discounts for bulk purchases for sales promo-
tions or premiums. Specific, large-quantity needs can be met with special editions, personalized covers, excerpts of existing guides, and corporate imprints.
For more information, contact:

Special Markets Department
DK Publishing, Inc.
375 Hudson Street
New York, NY 10014
Fax: 212-689-5254

Cataloging-in-Publication data is available
from the Library of Congress
ISBN 0-7566-0057-x

Printed in the UK by Butler & Tanner Limited

First printing, October 2004

LEXINGTON

Thoroughbred yearlings cavort at the
Diamond A Farms in the rolling hills of
Bluegrass country.
Photo by David Robertson

KENTUCKY 24/7

24 Hours. 7 Days.
Extraordinary Images of
One Week in Kentucky.

Created by Rick Smolan and David Elliot Cohen

DK Publishing

About the America 24/7 Project

A hundred years hence, historians may pose questions such as: What was America like at the beginning of the third millennium? How did life change after 9/11 and the ensuing war on terrorism? How was America affected by its corporate scandals and the high-tech boom and bust? Could Americans still express themselves freely?

To address these questions, we created *America 24/7*, the largest collaborative photography event in history. We invited Americans to tell their stories with digital pictures. We asked them to shoot a visual memoir of their lives, families, and communities.

During one week in May 2003, more than 25,000 professionals and amateurs shot more than a million pictures. These images, sent to us via the Internet, compose a panoramic yet highly intimate view of Americans in celebration and sadness; in action and contemplation; at work, home, and school. The best of these photographs, more than 6,000, are collected in 51 volumes that make up the *America 24/7* series: the landmark national volume *America 24/7*, published to critical acclaim in 2003, and the 50 state books published in 2004.

Our decision to make *America 24/7* an all-digital project was prompted by the fact that in 2003 digital camera sales overtook film camera sales. This techno-logical evolution allowed us to extend the project to a huge pool of photographers. We were thrilled by the response to our challenge and moved by the insight offered into American life. Sometimes, the amateurs outshot the pros—even the Pulitzer Prize winners.

The exuberant democracy of images visible throughout these books is a revela-tion. The message that emerges is that now, more than ever, America is a supersized idea. A dreamspace, where individuals and families from around the world are free to govern themselves, worship, read, and speak as they wish. Within its wide margins, the polyglot American nation manages to encompass an inexplicably complex yet workable whole. The pictures in this book are dedicated to that idea.

—*Rick Smolan and David Elliot Cohen*

American nightlight: More than a quarter of a billion people trace a nation with incandescence in this composite satellite photograph.
Photo by Craig Mayhew & Robert Simmon, NASA Goddard Flight Center/Visions of Tomorrow

My Old Kentucky Home

By Al Cross

Kentucky is a commonwealth of contrasts. Celebrated for its many elite pleasures (Thoroughbred horses, fine bourbon whiskeys, and the annual Festival of New American Plays in Louisville) Kentucky also has more than its share of poverty and ignorance, which makes it the occasional butt of late-night television jokes.

The real Kentucky, pictured in these pages, is somewhere in between. It's a state of hard-working folk, whose cleverness and toughness are exemplified by Bill Monroe and Colonel Harland Sanders, who not only invented bluegrass music and Kentucky Fried Chicken but made them international phenomena. The state is also home to Hall of Fame shortstop Pee Wee Reese, who, by embracing teammate Jackie Robinson, helped overcome racial prejudice. The great Muhammad Ali suffered racism as a child in Louisville, but the man has given the city a center that will celebrate his dramatic life and promote his values of peace and social responsibility.

Our state is an amalgam of North and South. It was a slave state that did not secede but joined the losing side after the Civil War because of what it considered shabby treatment by the Union, with one gripe being that slave-holders were not reimbursed for their freed slaves. Kentucky's metropolitan areas are now more tied to the Midwest and the East, but it remains a place where the accents are mostly Southern.

Life in Kentucky is shaped by the land. The Thoroughbreds grazing in the Bluegrass near the heart of Kentucky are the state's leading agricultural product and the main reason Lexington is a tourist destination. On the state's northern border, towns and cities line the Ohio River, America's first great thoroughfare and still a key lifeline. Eastward are the Appalachian Mountains, suffering from relative isolation and the economic vagaries and environmental risks of coal mining. To the west and south are a flat coalfield and a swath of tobacco, cattle, corn, and soybean farms that bespeak the essentially rural nature of Kentucky. (In the region's 1st Congressional District, the tallest building in Hopkinsville, the largest city, is a grain elevator.) In most places, life revolves around courthouse towns, of which there are many, because Kentucky has more than its share of counties—120 for 4 million people. Ask Kentuckians where they're from, and they're as likely to name a county as a city.

Through most of the 20th century, Kentucky changed less than other states and fell behind. In-migration was light and out-migration was heavy as natives left for better jobs. In a sense, people were Kentucky's leading export. The state still ranks high in native-born population, but that's changing: The 1990s saw education reforms, more people moving in than moving out, and a sharp decline of the tobacco culture that shored up small-town economies and small-farm values. That evolution has also made Kentucky a leading auto manufacturer.

Still, as Kentuckians have migrated to new factory towns and metros, they yet have faith that their country home remains a special place in the heart of America.

Al Cross *is the political writer and columnist for The Courier-Journal in Louisville and former president of the Society of Professional Journalists.*

LOUISVILLE

At dawn, a barge loaded with ore, petroleum products, steel, and iron is pushed up the Ohio River past Louisville by the towboat *Queen City*. The Ingram Barge Company is one of 30 that plies the river, transporting 239 million tons of cargo a year.

Photo by David R. Lutman

HYDEN

Be prepared: Boy Scout Brandon Douglas Collins, flag bearer for Troop 501, gets ready for opening ceremonies at the American Cancer Society's Relay for Life.

Photo by Chad Allen Stevens, Western Kentucky University

LOUISVILLE

"We were raised to bless the food before we eat," says Amanda Smith. She and her husband Albert dine at Jay's Cafeteria after Sunday services at Shiloh Baptist Church. The West End restaurant has served family-style meals like catfish, greens, and mashed potatoes since 1974.

Photo by Sam Upshaw, Jr.

WHITESBURG

"Buddy, if a big one takes it, you think your rod's going to break," says Eddie Johnson, who drives to Fish Pond Lake two mornings a week to try his luck fishing for trout.

Photo by Chad Allen Stevens, Western Kentucky University

ROSINE

Hometown to bluegrass pioneer Bill Monroe, Rosine has porchfuls of residents who follow faithfully in his path. Here, Ed Edwards, Bill Burden, Blake Render, Josh Johnston, and Chris Edwards let loose with their twangy, Gaelic rhythms on the porch of the Rosine General Store.

Photo by Pam Spaulding

GLASGOW

Construction worker Bryan Buford hoists his 4-month-old son, Stephen, above the disarray of the house he shares with Andrea Stonerock and their children. When Buford and Stonerock met, they discovered they each had 5-year-olds born on the same day. The chemistry extended beyond the coincidence, and several months later the couple moved in together.

Photo by Bill Luster, The Courier-Journal

Hearth & Home

LOUISVILLE

It's 6:50 a.m. and Hayden Dry faces another day of classes at Kentucky Country School where the bell rings at 8:00 a.m. sharp.
Photo by Dan Dry

LOUISVILLE

Since adopting Lily and Rose from Shaowu and Nanning, China, Jeri McDonogh and her husband have made the girls' culture a priority, celebrating Chinese New Year, attending Chinese classes with their daughters, and reading bedtime stories about the country. In Louisville, 150 families have joined the McDonoghs' support group for parents of adopted Chinese children.
Photo by Pat McDonogh

BOWLING GREEN

Just a year after moving to Bowling Green from Chicago, Sunnie, the golden retriever, has quickly adjusted to laid-back southern life. In a bedroom the size of her old city yard, Sunnie joins owner David Adams-Smith for a nap.

Photo by Jeanie Adams-Smith,
Western Kentucky University

MIDWAY

Jair Pedroza and his family live on Pin Oak Stud farm where housing is part of the pay package for his job as stallion manager. When not feeding, exercising, or breeding the horses, Pedroza accompanies his wife Claudia and their children Sagnitte, Samantha, and Jair Jr. for outings on the 3,100-acre farm.
Photo by Dan Dry

MANCHESTER

"I love these hills," says Bobby Deaton, 71. He retired to Florida in 1956 but moved back in 1988. "I live at the home place now—where I grew up, where my grandparents lived."

Photo by Chad Allen Stevens,
Western Kentucky University

BOWLING GREEN

"We planned to have kids some day, but we weren't expecting to start so soon, and with so many!" says Vanessa Menjivar, who was 20 years old when she discovered she was pregnant with quadruplets. She gave birth to Leandro, Miguel, Gabriella, and Joseph at 25 weeks. The children were in prenatal intensive care for three months. *Photos by Jeanie Adams-Smith, Western Kentucky University*

BOWLING GREEN

The Menjivars go through three gallons of milk each day. Bottles—on the windowsill, in the refrigerator, and on the counter—are always ready for that first cry for milk, soon followed by three more distinctive wails.

BOWLING GREEN

With a shoe for every occasion, the quadruplets learned to walk in style, aided by a mom who understood exactly what they were going through. After her pregnancy, Vanessa contracted a virus that left her lower body paralyzed for six months. "I learned to walk again at the same time as my children," she says.

Yes Sir, That's My Baby: Newlyweds Michelle and Michael Elliott take to the dance floor at their wedding reception. "We didn't want a traditional wedding," says Michelle. The couple rented a 1920s mansion for the ceremony and reception, took Charleston dance lessons, and hired a red-hot jazz band.

Photos by David R. Lutman

LOUISVILLE

In a Roaring 20s send-off, Carol and Mitchell Matthews (best man) wait outside the Frazier House for the newlyweds to leave for their honeymoon. Carol and other close friends had their hair and makeup done by a professional stylist to get them properly rouged and bobbed.

LOUISVILLE

Father of the bride Danny Brannon kindles his own romance. After the toast, he and girlfriend Deborah Falkowski smooch in the sitting room.

COVINGTON

Donna and Arthur Barker tie the knot on the *Belle of Cincinnati*, moored on the Ohio River. "Our ceremony was on the top level of the boat, overlooking downtown Cincinnati," says Arthur, operations manager for a trucking company. "It was a good start." Donna's daughter Kristen and Justice of the Peace Stephen Hoffman agree.
Photo by Patrick Reddy, Cincinnati Enquirer

COWAN

Just a few hours before Chris (in foreground) and Hannah Miles exchanged vows at the Cowan Community Center, the entrance to the hall was knee-deep in mud from heavy rains. Two women from the center rolled up their sleeves, got out their push brooms, and cleared the way for the wedding party.
Photo by Chad Allen Stevens, Western Kentucky University

LOUISVILLE

"My friends like to say I'm the only girl they know who had to move to New York to meet a boy from home," says Blair Shelby. She and her husband Thom moved to New York about five years ago. The two were home visiting family when friends introduced them. Five flower girls later...

Photo by Dan Dry

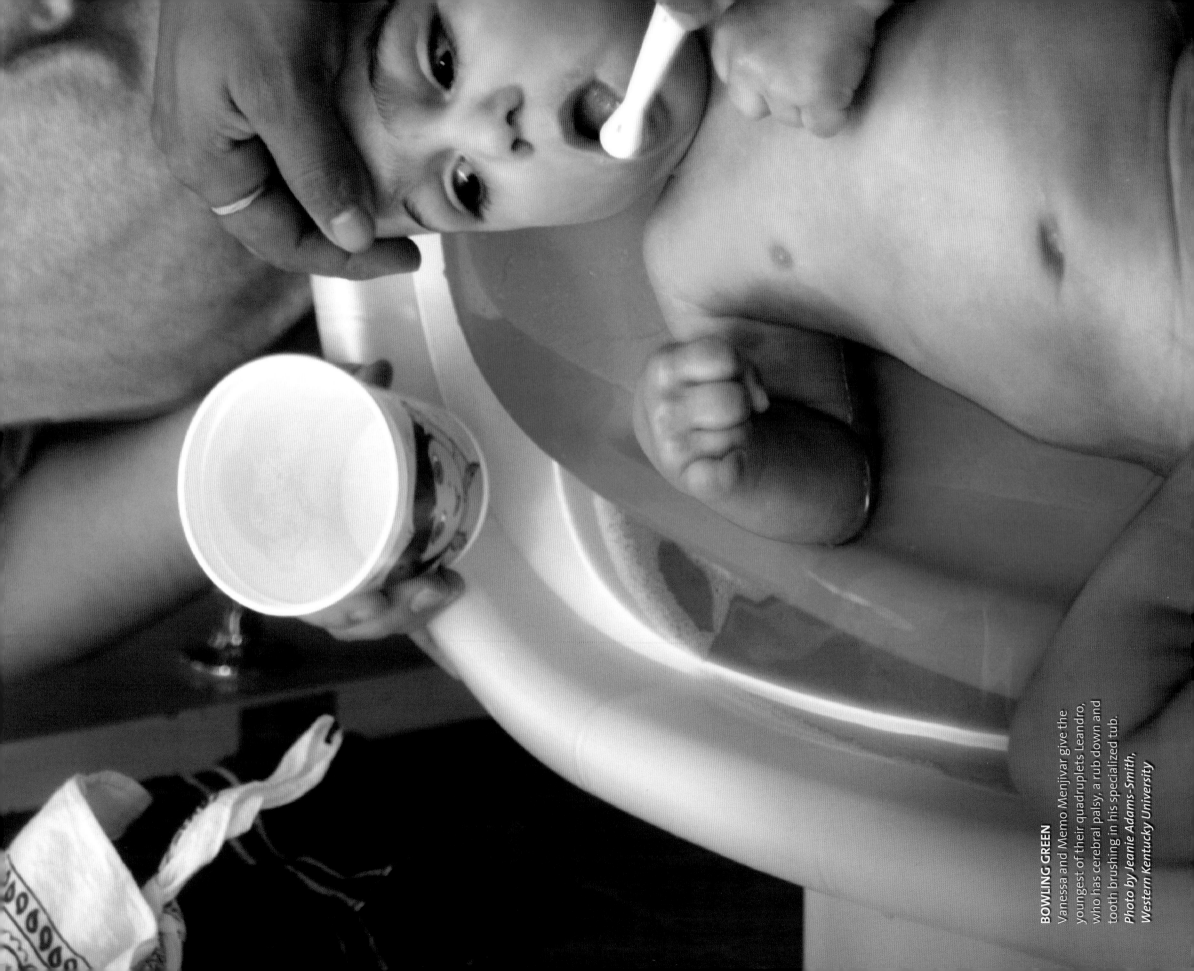

BOWLING GREEN
Vanessa and Memo Menjivar give the
youngest of their quadruplets Leandro,
who has cerebral palsy, a rub down and
tooth brushing in his specialized tub.
Photo by Jeanie Adams-Smith,
Western Kentucky University

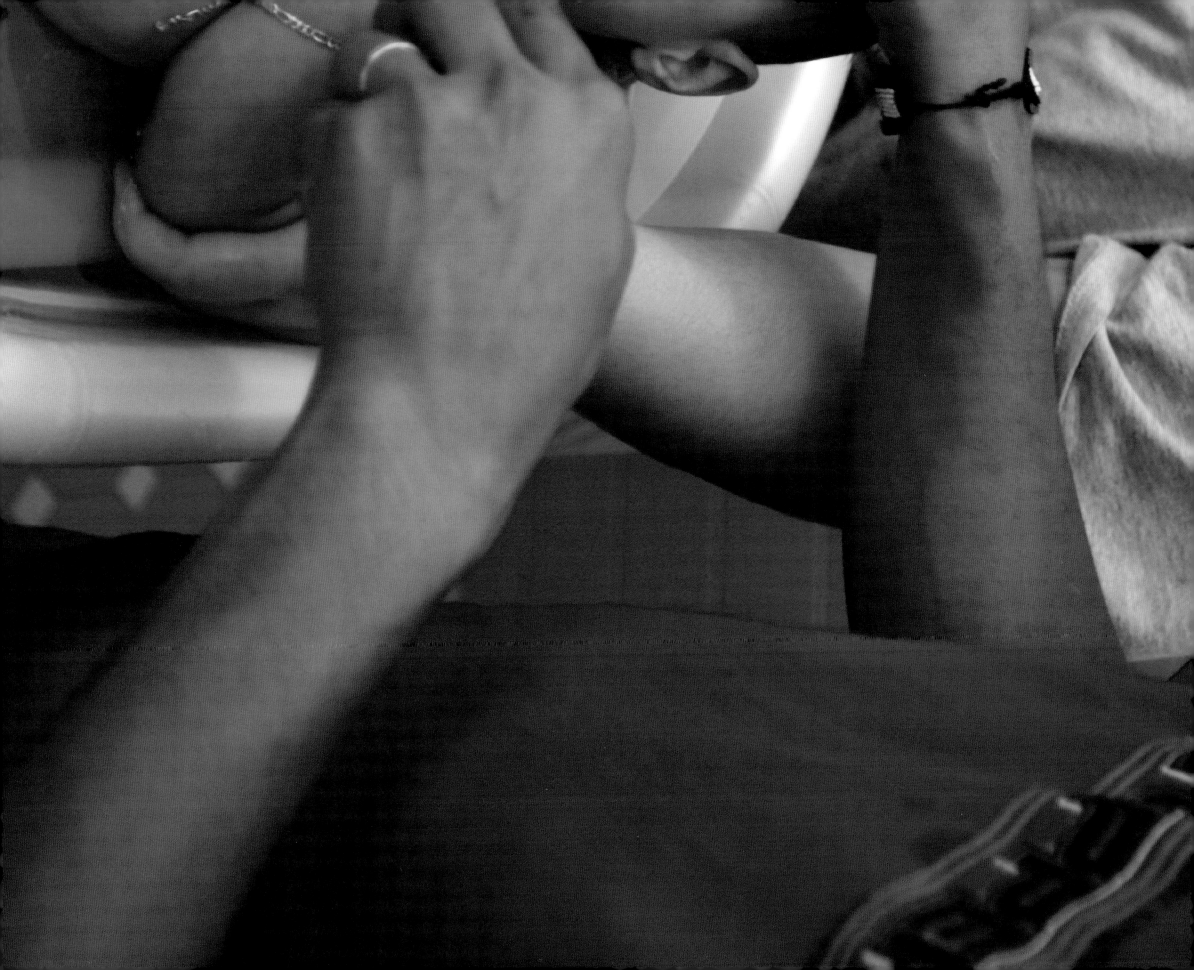

BOWLING GREEN

The mother of six, Pam Lipp says she always has at least one child around. As she puts on makeup in the bathroom, she's joined by 1-year-old Jacob.

Photos by James H. Kenney,
Western Kentucky University

BOWLING GREEN

The Lipp children gather around the kitchen table for class. Before cracking the books, mom leads them through the Pledge of Allegiance, religious prayers, and games. She began homeschooling in 1995, when her oldest daughter Theresa (now in college) was entering middle school. "I wanted her to have a better learning environment," she explains.

BOWLING GREEN

Reading, writing, and arithmetic make up the basic curriculum in the Lipp home. When they're not in school, the children play on community sports teams, participate in church events, and attend parties sponsored by the Barren River Home Schooling Association. Kentucky has 12,490 registered homeschoolers.

HOPKINSVILLE

At 17, Wyoming native Rebecca Ochs moved to Hopkinsville with her boyfriend and got married. Today, Ochs, 28, is a mom of two boys. "Since I was a little girl, I knew I wanted a husband and children," she says. "If I died tomorrow, I wouldn't feel I'd missed anything."

Photos by Jeanie Adams-Smith,
Western Kentucky University

HOPKINSVILLE

Since Justuce Ochs's father works long hours as a truck driver, the 7-year-old hangs out with his neighborly father figure, Bruce Bell, from whose window he peers out.

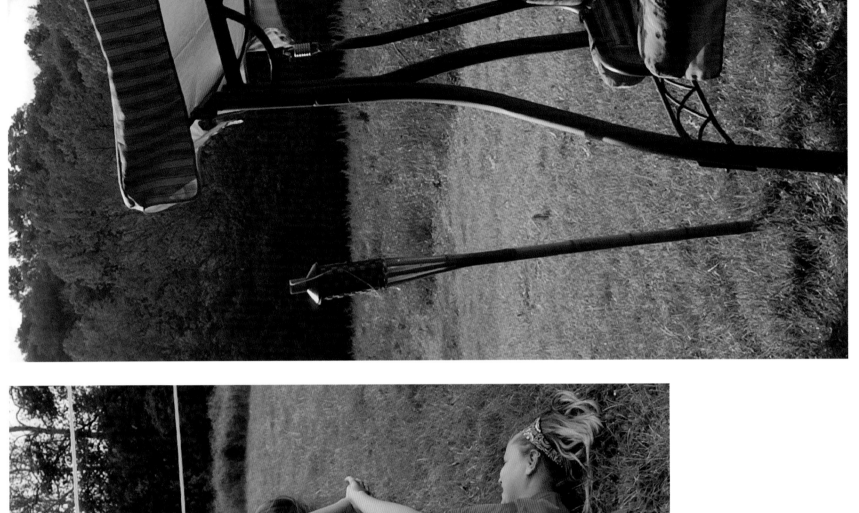

BEDFORD

Becky Adams tumbles over her cousin Kayla Turocy. Becky and Kayla's household includes six siblings and cousins, ages 5 to 16. There are always plenty of playmates.

Photos by Bill Luster, The Courier-Journal

BEDFORD

Kayla Turocy reads so much that she often stays on the sofa swing until well after sunset. Torches illuminate her nighttime literary journeys.

LOUISVILLE

Second-grader Adam Tuma always eats breakfast with his backpack on so he won't forget it in his rush to catch the school bus.

Photo by Bill Luster, The Courier-Journal

Hush up! Brock Shively joined the grown-ups to celebrate the 20th birthday of his nanny Sara McGarvey (head bowed). Like most 4-year-olds, he has trouble staying quiet for the blessing.
Photo by Pam Spaulding

GLASGOW

Bryan Buforc relishes feeding his son Stephen. "I do it when I wake up, when I come home from work, when Stephen wakes in the middle of the night," he says. "It's what we do together."
Photo by Bill Luster, The Courier-Journal

LINE FORK

Lee Sexton, 75, bought his first banjo at the age of 7 with the dollar he earned cutting a field of corn stalks. He has since composed classics such as "Cumberland Gap" and "Little Birdie." Featured in the film *Coal Miner's Daughter*, Sexton received the Governor's Award in the Arts in 1999.
Photo by Chad Allen Stevens, Western Kentucky University

LANCASTER

Haircuts and harmonies: During one of the many daily jams at Brummett & Todd's Barber Shop, co-owner Charlie Brummett picks a banjo, Ron Scott plays a guitar, and Wesley Pingleton, 15, bows a fiddle.

Photo by David Stephenson

The year 2003 marked a turning point in the history of photography: it was the first year that digital cameras outsold film cameras. To celebrate this unprecedented sea change, the *America 24/7* project invited amateur photographers—along with students and professionals—to shoot and, via the Internet, submit digital images. Think of it as audience participation. Their visions of community are interspersed with the professional frames throughout this book. On the following four pages, however, we present a gallery produced exclusively by amateur photographers.

HENDERSON This 3-foot garden statue is tucked into the museum grounds at John James Audobon Park, which honors favorite son Audobon, who spent much of his life in Henderson. *Photo by Jeff Osborne*

LOUISVILLE The lion tunnel at the Louisville Zoo frames Quincy Dye and David Leitz. The boys just finished touring the zoo's new gorilla exhibit. *Photo by Michael Leitz*

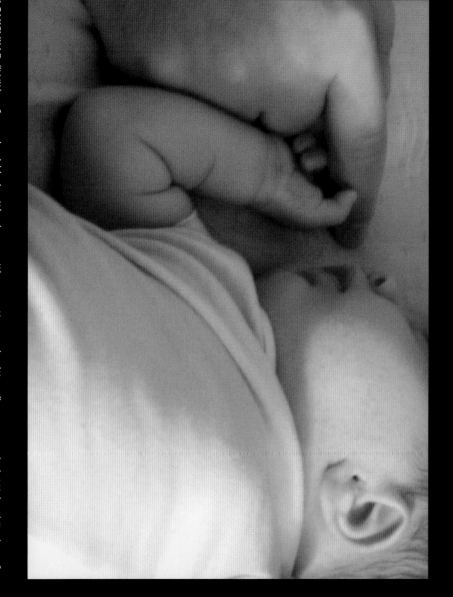

LOUISVILLE "With a 6-week-old baby, it's always either naptime or bedtime," says new dad, Michael Tucker of his daughter Sierra. *Photo by Michael Tucker*

LOUISVILLE Isabella Letson Ettin peers into her father's camera while hanging from the jungle gym bars at Tyler Park. *Photo by Douglas Ettin*

LEXINGTON Run with the roses: Life-size bronze horses stampede across Thoroughbred Park in downtown Lexington. The monument was sculpted by Gwen Reardon in 1992. *Photo by David Nash*

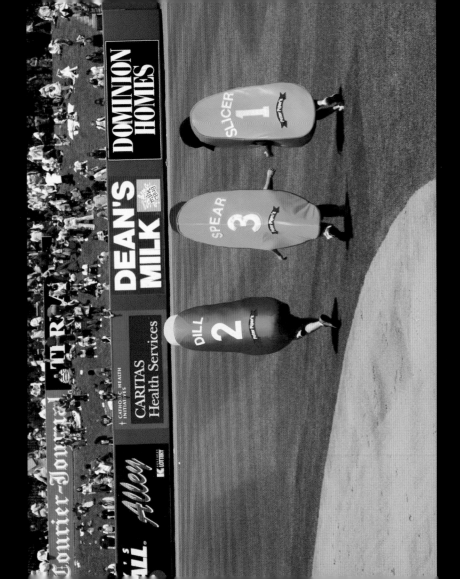

LOUISVILLE Fans at Slugger Field are entertained by Dean Foods' human pickles during the seventh-inning stretch. The Louisville Bats beat the Pawtucket Red Sox 7–3. *Photo by Kenneth Gantz*

GEORGETOWN No one's sure if Sammy was abandoned or ran away, but when the husky-m x puppy showed ...he found his way into photographer Katie Palnk's home and heart. *Photo by Katie Palnk*

VALLEY VIEW The Valley View Ferry, which began service in 1785 and is the oldest business in Kentucky, links Fayette and Jessamine counties to Madison County across the Kentucky River. *Photo by David Nash*

MCALPINE LOCKS, OHIO RIVER

Deckhand Jared Payne ratchets the wire that connects the hoppers on a barge. The *O.H. Ingram* towboat pushes the loaded barge upriver from the Newburgh Locks to the McAlpine Locks.

Photo by David R. Lutman

LEXINGTON

That feels good! A race horse gets a bath after its morning workout. Grooms say the horses like the suds because they're salty.

Photo by David Robertson

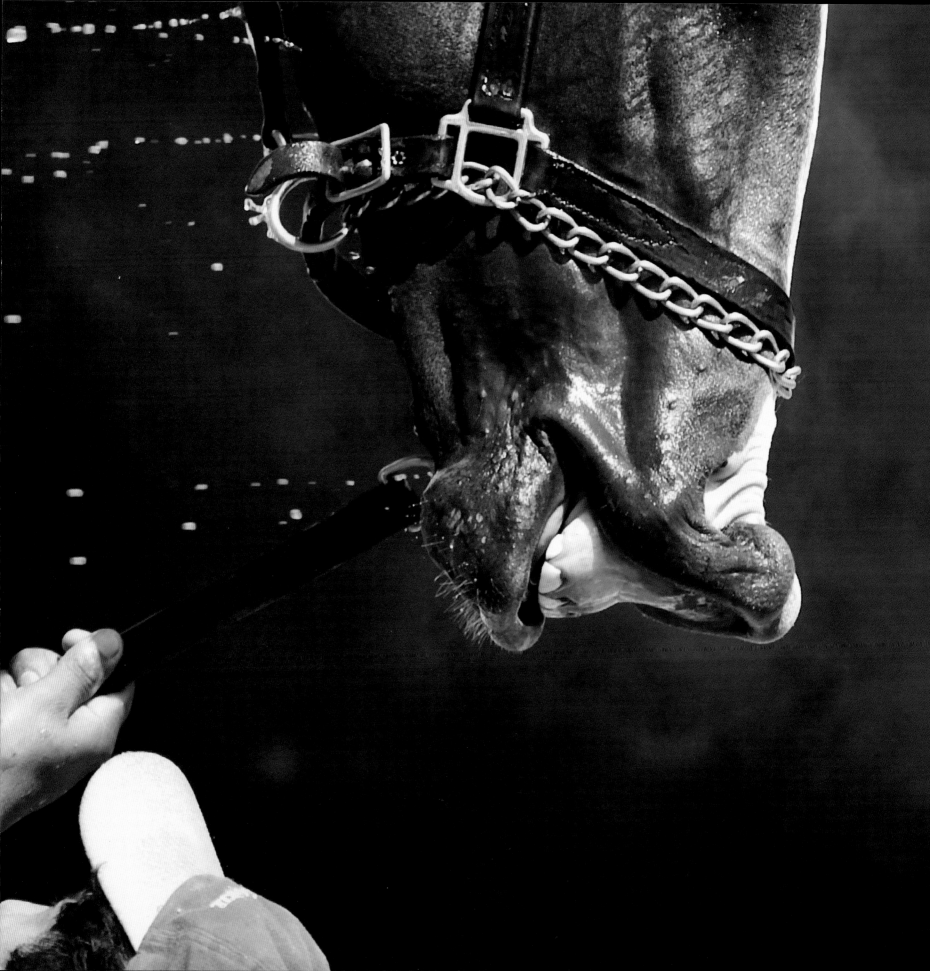

LEXINGTON

At the hospital, Cole Begley, a vet tech student at Murray State, tends to a surgical patient. To prevent the foal from standing up, Begley leans on its neck.
Photo by Bill Luster, The Courier-Journal

LEXINGTON

At the Rood and Riddle Equine Hospital, Dr. Rolf Embertson and Dr. Brady Bergin perform a transphyseal bridge surgery to temporarily stop the growth of one side of a yearling's limb, which is developing too quickly. Founded in 1986, the hospital treats horses from all over the country.
Photo by Bill Luster, The Courier-Journal

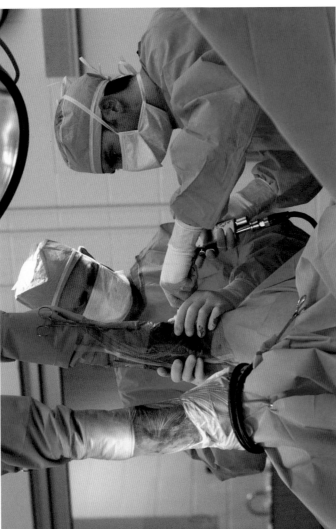

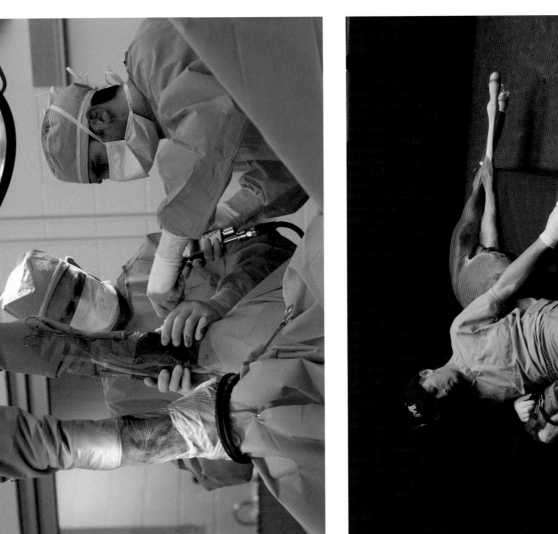

MIDWAY

After earning his owners $1,589,270 during his racing career, Pin Oak Stud farm's stallion Peaks and Valleys gets *his* reward—three times a day, from February through June. Farm manager, Clifford Barry (second from left) and his team supervise the race horse's efforts with In By Six.

Photo by Dan Dry

LOUISVILLE

Ever since Greta Kuntzweiler saw *The Black Stallion* in third grade, she knew she wanted to build her life around horses. At 12, she got her first pony. At 18, she began racing competitively. Today, at 27, she is one of three regular female riders at the prestigious Churchill Downs track, which opened with the Kentucky Derby in 1875.
Photos by Bill Luster, The Courier-Journal

LOUISVILLE
After a muddy race at Churchill Downs, jockey Shelley Moran weighs in. At 105 pounds, Moran, whose mother Betty Moran was one of the first female jockeys, often has to load her saddle with lead pads to bring her up to the 122-pound weight requirement for races.

LOUISVILLE

Jockey Greta Kuntzweiler steers Banker Wallace to the finish line. In her nine-year racing career, Kuntzweiler has broken her ankle, back, and shoulder but never once considered giving up the sport.

Photo by Bill Luster, The Courier-Journal

LANCASTER

Kentucky has the largest number of beef cattle east of the Mississippi, with more than one million head. In 2003, the Garrard County Stock Yards moved 60,000. The auction house, which opened in the early 1900s, holds sales every Friday.

Photo by David Stephenson

LEXINGTON

The McCracken family uses a row setter to plant tobacco seedlings. Federally mandated production quotas reduced Kentucky's tobacco harvest from 470 million pounds in 1997 to 204 million pounds in 2003 and have shrunk profits for small farmers like Randy and Kathy McCracken. They have had to get second jobs to make ends meet.

Photo by Charles Bertram

WHITESBURG

Since retiring from the coal mines in 1991, David Dinsmore has been growing potatoes and mustard greens for his family. Backyard farming "got less pleasant" in 2000, when mining resumed on nearby Black Mountain, says Dinsmore. He now sees coal and construction dust in the air, on his crops, and in local streams.

Photo by Charles Bertram

PINE HILL

From 1920 to 1969, Mail Pouch Tobacco Company painted its slogan on 10,000 barns in America. Owners were paid in cash, magazine subscriptions, or chewing tobacco. They also had the rest of their barn painted. But nowadays, "barns like this are getting scarcer than hen's teeth," says Thomas Benton Miller, whose family has owned this barn since 1960.

Photo by Charles Bertram

WILLIAMSBURG

Kentucky has the largest percentage of smokers (32.6 percent) in America. That's why Joe Jones opened a drive-up tobacco shack on Highway 25, the fourth such shop in Williamsburg. Jones sells all kinds of tobacco, including some brands that are only available in Kentucky. The shop is open seven days a week and sold approximately $700,000 worth of smokes in 2003.

Photo by John Isaac

FRANKFORT

Master Distiller Emeritus Elmer T. Lee checks on the aging barrels at Buffalo Trace Distillery. The company, which has been making bourbon since 1787, requires that these barrels be made from the center rings of 80-year-old American white oaks and that they be charred inside to a depth of one-eighth inch, for that smoky flavor.

Photos by Ron Garrison

FRANKFORT

After tasting bourbon for 50 years, Lee has developed a sharp palate. One of 10 tasters at the distillery, he looks for a specific flavor profile. "You can't learn this in a book or over the Internet," he says. "The only way is on the job."

Kentucky produces 43 million gallons of bourbon a year—95 percent of the world's total. At Labrot & Graham Distillery, tourists watch a tub of bourbon mash (corn, rye, malted barley, and yeast) ferment.

As it passes in front of the inspection light, Barbara Hippe checks a one-liter bottle of Labrot & Graham's Woodford Reserve to make sure it is free of "floaters" (cork dust) and other imperfections. Woodford Reserve is the best-selling super-premium bourbon in the state and the official bourbon of the Kentucky Derby.

LOUISVILLE

In 1990, Bardstown native Eddie Miles quit his job as a mail carrier to pursue his dream of producing a traveling Elvis tribute show. In the years since, he has performed everywhere from Thailand to Ireland and now awaits his curtain call at the Brown Theater in Louisville. Miles averages 100 shows a year; his repertoire includes 250 Elvis songs.

Photos by Pat McDonogh

LOUISVILLE

Eddie Miles reviews his pompadour during a break in his Elvis tribute. One of 35,000 Elvis impersonators worldwide, Miles attributes the success of his show to its tastefulness. "I may dress like Elvis," he says, "but I'm not one of those guys who goes out there saying, 'I'm the King.'"

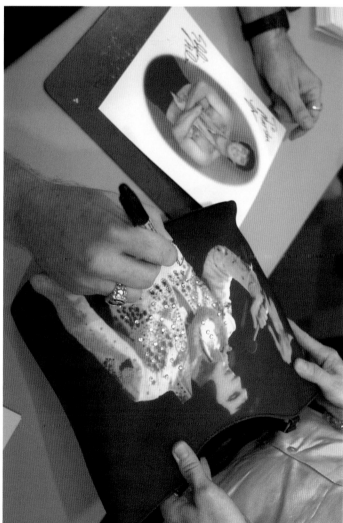

LOUISVILLE

After two and a half hours performing before a full house at the Brown Theater, Miles signs souvenirs of himself as Elvis.

BOWLING GREEN

Jack Fish, 76, takes his bicycle down the elevator in his apartment building to deliver the *Park City Daily News*. He lost his job as a shipping clerk in 1996 and took the daily paper route to pay the bills. "I don't know anyone who can do it on just Social Security," he says.

Photos by James H. Kenney,
Western Kentucky University

BOWLING GREEN

One of the things Fish likes about his delivery job is the people and pets he meets along the way. "This ol' girl, her name is Ebony," he says. "Her tail starts wagging as soon as she sees my bike. Then, we kiss and shake hands."

BOWLING GREEN

The newspaper company delivers the papers to Fish's apartment; then, he rolls and bags 'em. On Sundays, after finishing the 90-minute route, he heads to the Fountain Square Methodist Church to play drums with the four-piece Worship Team. "I'm not great, but I enjoy it, and it's the only way I can stay awake in church," he says.

BEREA

Berea College was established in 1855 to provide an education for poor, academically promising Appalachian students. That mission continues today. To support the school, its 1,500 students work 10 hours a week on campus. Jessica Culver has a job in the weaving department; her blankets and rugs are sold online and at crafts fairs.

Photo by David Stephenson

LEXINGTON

Even at 99, Thomas D. Clark continues working. Kentucky's historian laureate has written dozens of books, created the state archives, and taught history at the University of Kentucky. He still writes on a Remington typewriter and works at home to be close to his second wife Loretta. They married when he was 92.

Photo by Charles Bertram

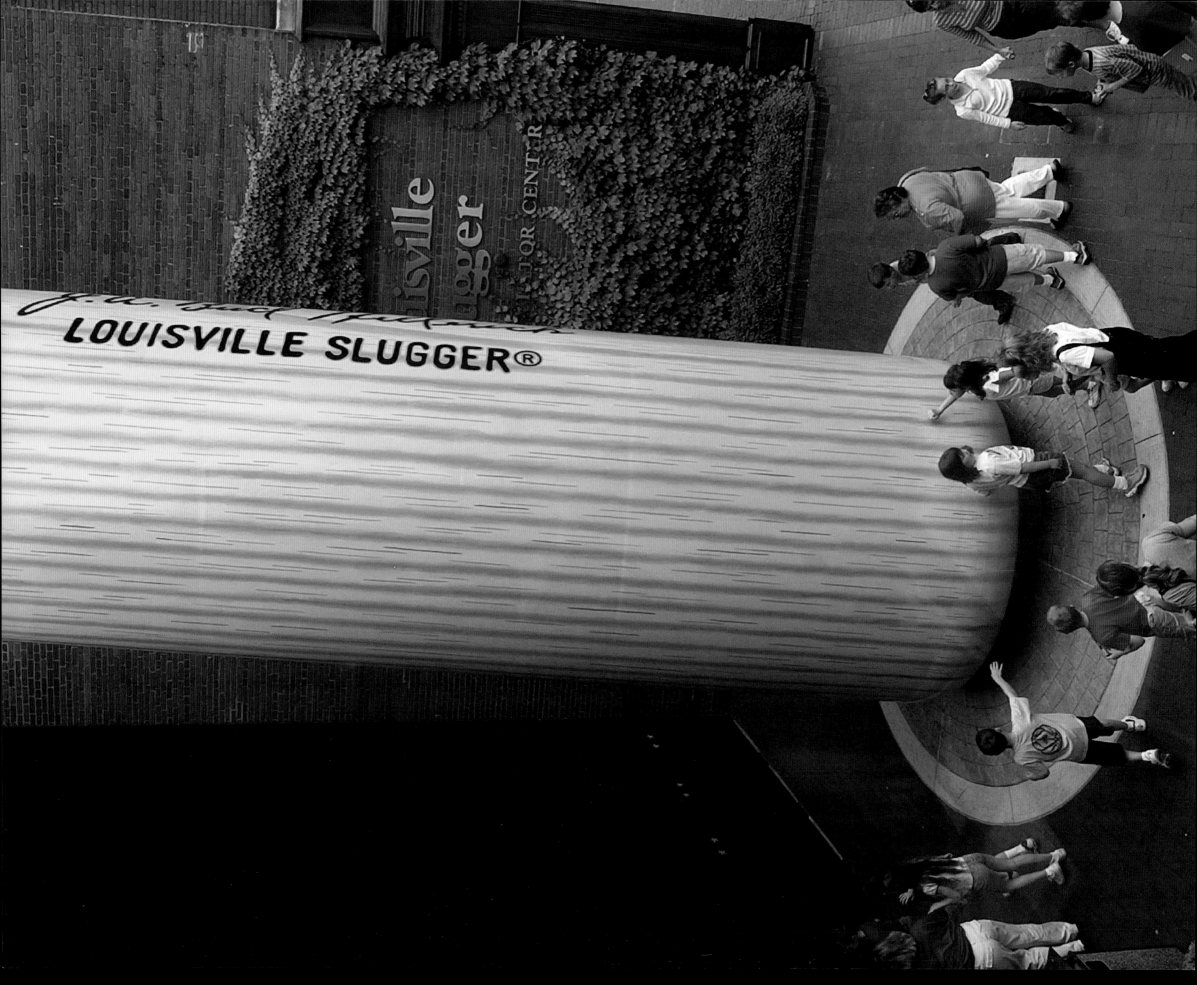

LOUISVILLE

A 120-foot baseball bat dominates the entrance of Hillerich & Bradsby, manufacturer of the Louisville Slugger, official bat of Major League Baseball. Founded in 1884, the company produces one million bats each year made from northern white ash.

Photos by Pat McDonogh

LOUISVILLE

In his 34 years with the company, Daniel Luckett has chiseled 40-by-3-inch billets into sleek Sluggers for most major leaguers from Hank Aaron to Pete Rose. In an eight-hour day, Luckett can produce 32 bats.

LOUISVILLE

A batch of freshly branded Louisville Sluggers awaits glazing. Professional players, who make up 70 percent of Hillerich & Bradsby's business, go through 100 of the $23 bats each year.

LOUISVILLE

Noted sculptor Ed Hamilton works on a "concept study" for an 8-foot, full-figure statue of York, the stalwart slave Lewis and Clark took on their epic expedition in 1803. "Some people's history didn't make it into the books," says Hamilton, who is glad to be part of a local effort to memorialize York with a prominent statue on the Louisville riverfront.

Photo by Sam Upshaw, Jr.

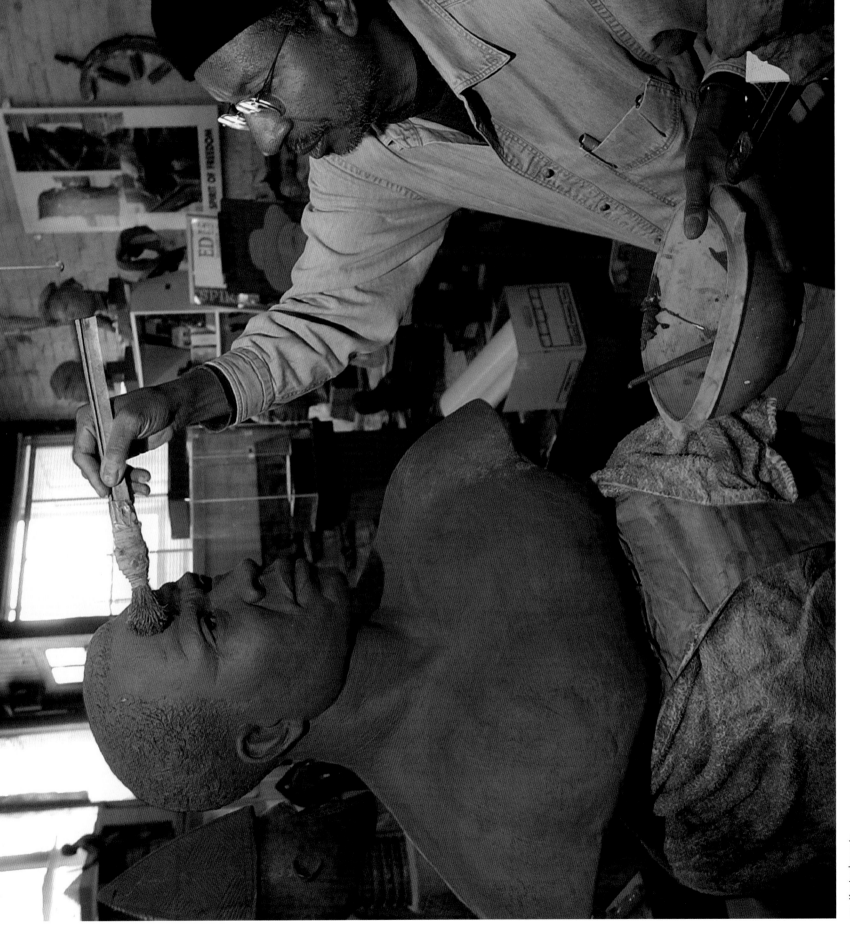

BOWLING GREEN

Artist Donnie Firkins refines facial details on a clay sculpture of a sailor, based on his model, Carlos Roque. Part of a series of four life-sized statues representing the four branches of the military, the ceramic molds will be cast in bronze and stand at the county courthouse to memorialize Warren County's veterans.

Photo by Jim Roshan, jimroshan.com

PADUCAH

The Paducah Floodwall Mural has been underway for seven years. On 20-foot-wide panels, Herb Roe paints a scene illustrating the area's history. "The Lewis and Clark expedition passed through here," says Roe of the panel's subject. "Clark came back and named the town for an Indian chief."

Photo by Jim Roshan, jimroshan.com

FLOYD COUNTY

This battery-powered vehicle takes Bruce Sparks, James Newsome, Larry Stevens, Dwayne Marsilett, Clinton Clatworthy (at the wheel), and Mitchell Crager 2,000 feet underground for their shift at North Star Mine. The mine gave up 393,000 tons of coal in 2003, helping to make Kentucky the third-largest coal producer in America.

Photos by John Isaac

HARLAN

Serving "any meal, any time," the Huddle House on South Main Street is a favorite with local miners. Rick Sage, Jack Webb, and Carson Whitehead down some coffee at 2 a.m., after their shift at Darby Fork Mine.

HARLAN

Six days a week, from 3:30 p.m. to 1:30 a.m., Rick Sage works six miles underground in an area that's 50 inches high. He started working in the mines after high school and knows it's dangerous: His father has second-stage black lung disease (it kills 1,500 coal miners a year). "Mining is all we know around here," Sage says.

BOWLING GREEN

A member of UAW Local 2164, Marvin Bundy mounts tires on the assembly line.

BOWLING GREEN

It takes 33 hours to put a Corvette together. Gayle Pawlawski installs a control arm on the suspension line of a Vette chassis. The Bowling Green plant is the third location to build the popular sports car since General Motors produced the first hand-built, dual-exhaust Polc White Roadster in Flint, Michigan, in 1953.

Photos by Jim Roshan, jimroshan.com

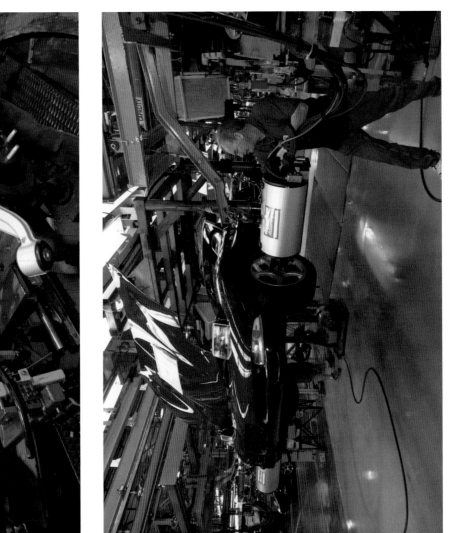

BOWLING GREEN

Most days, the Bowling Green plant turns out 150 Corvettes. These fifth-generation models (the same style has been produced since 1997) are a few of the 35,000 Vettes that roll off the line each year.

FORT CAMPBELL

Preparing for their deployment to Iraq, an Army reserve unit conducts a MOUT exercise (military operation in urban terrain) on the Fort Campbell Army base. As they clear a building or evacuate an area, they are honing their skills for combat situations.

Photos by Jim Roshan, jimroshan.com

FORT CAMPBELL

On the first of 11 days at the Air Assault School, soldiers tackle 14 obstacles before a two-mile run. "It's known as the 11 hardest days you'll spend in the Army," says George Heath, public relations officer. "You have to reach down inside yourself to find levels of tolerance and grit you never knew you had."

LOUISVILLE
At the 40,000-square-foot Louisville Extreme Sports Park's concrete course, skaters perform nollies, mongo-foots, and McTwists.
Photo by Pat McDonogh

Kentucky At Play

CAVE RUN LAKE

Although they can be tricky for boaters, these submerged trees are perfect for catching muskie, which thrives in undergrowth. Known as the "Muskie Capital of the South," the lake, dammed in 1974, holds the record for the largest muskie caught in Kentucky. The 1998 whopper weighed 44 pounds, was 53 inches long, and had a girth of 26 inches.

Photo by Ron Garrison

MUDDY FORD

Mike Weaver shows off the bluegill he caught at a pond on a friend's farm. An avid fisherman, ace mathematician, and published photographer, Mike has big plans for his future. "I'm thinking about being an engineer, or maybe a doctor," he says. "I'll do photography on the side and, of course, spend plenty of time fishing."

Photo by Ken Weaver

LIVINGSTON

The little engine that could, or couldn't. Though the driver tried three times to master this hill, all he ended up with was a broken suspension. This area, a favorite for pushing all-terrain vehicles, jeeps, and motorcycles to their limits, is known as Pink Rock, for its blush-colored soil.

Photo by David Stephenson

RABBIT HASH

During a 90-mile training ride, cyclist Tony Franklin of Covington made a quick stop at the Rabbit Hash General Store, which has been operating since 1831. Local lore says the town, once a busy steamboat landing, was named for a dish served far too often after the Ohio River flooded and rabbits proliferated in the surrounding hills.

Photo by Patrick Reddy, Cincinnati Enquirer

SLADE

"The Red River Gorge is a magical place to climb," says Mindy Willis. After driving eight hours from Ontario, Canada, she and a cadre of friends spend the weekend testing their mettle on routes like the 120-foot Mule.

Photos by David Coyle

SLADE

Tom Hentschel, a former competitive body builder, leads a climb up the Fuzzy Undercling route along Military Wall. With more than a thousand recorded routes, "The Red" keeps rock climbers busy from dawn to dusk.

CAMPBELLSVILLE

Christopher Thomas and his sister Elydia take a break from after-school chores. Even though their parents work off the farm at General Electric and Taylor County Hospital, the family still manages to run a small business of dairy cows, hay, and tobacco on their 137-acre property.

Photo by Pam Spaulding

LOUISVILLE

Shlomie Litvin shoots baskets wearing his prayer shawl and skullcap, the garments worn at all times by Orthodox Jews. Son of Rabbi Av'ohom Litvin, Shlomie is comfortable keeping to his religious responsibilities and to being a kid at the same time.

Photo by David R. Lutman

HARLAN

To keep her edge, Alisha Curry spends time in the batting cage. Catcher and clean-up hitter on her undefeated Little League team, the seventh-grader has been drafted to play with the older girls on the Harlan Dragons high school team.

Photo by Charles Bertram

BOWLING GREEN

Larry Kessinger drove 60 miles from Center Town to catch his grandson Wyatt's first T-ball match. He caught most of it.
Photo by Tim Broekema,
Western Kentucky University

LEXINGTON

Shortstop John Weaver of the undefeated Dodgers, a Babe Ruth League team, tags Yankee Thomas Price. "I love everything about baseball," says Weaver, who practices hitting four times a week during winter and hopes to play pro ball.
Photo by Ken Weaver

Veterinarian Karen Thomason whistles commands to Quill, her border collie. "You might ask him to do something specific, but the sheep move so quickly, you have to trust that he'll do what works," says Thomason. "A border collie is more than a pet."

LEXINGTON

The Bluegrass Classic Open Stock Dog Trial at Masterson Station Park assembles some of the top herding dogs in the country. "Only the border collie can do what we ask of these dogs," says Melinda Hanley, an event organizer. "They've been bred to it for centuries."

Photos by Ken Weaver

LEXINGTON

Quill cuts four sheep out of the herd during the annual stock dog trials. The competition simulates chores on a working farm: separating an injured animal, gathering sheep into the barn, or penning them for sale. The dog has to have enough power to gain respect from the sheep without frightening them.

BOWLING GREEN

Josh Harwood, 13, pilots his hand-built car in an elimination heat at the Bowling Green Soap Box Derby. "It's a family event to put a car together, and the kids love to show them off," says Brent Brennerstuhl, the event's organizer. Boys and girls ages 8 to 17 compete in 130 cities for a spot at the national championship in Ohio.

Photo by Tim Broekema, Western Kentucky University

MT. VERNON

After the Burr Hill truck stop burned down, Charles Mink (far rear) turned the rickety ruin into a shooting gallery. James Barron (taking aim) and others gather between 5 p.m. and midnight on most Fridays and Saturdays. Mink supplies the modified 12-gauge shotguns and everyone puts $10 into the pool. The best marksman of the night gets the pot.

Photo by David Stephenson

SALYERSVILLE

A popular hangout, the Barn is a pool hall *and* drive-through liquor store—folks literally drive through the building and runners deliver orders to customers' cars. The pool hall is also a favorite among local contractors. "You can always find guys ready to play a game," says Joshua "Doc" Holliday, lining up a shot on a visit from George-town, Kentucky.

Photo by John Isaac

SACRAMENTO

On December 28, 1861, a Confederate force led
by Colonel Nathan Bedford Forrest and informed
by Confederate sympathizer Mollie Morehead,
defeated the Union troops in Sacramento. Civil
War buffs reenact the Battle of Sacramento with
mock battles, cannon ball blasts, a pageant, and
fashion show.

*Photo by Jeanie Adams-Smith,
Western Kentucky University*

MAMMOTH CAVES

Adventurers descend 160 feet along Frozen
Niagara, one of several limestone formations
in Mammoth Caves. With more than 350 miles
explored and mapped, this is the most extensive
cave system in the world. The caves provided
saltpeter for the production of gunpowder in
the 1800s; today, they are visited by more than
500,000 tourists a year.

Photo by Patrick L. Pfister, pjfoto.com

LIBERTY

Founded in 1985 by Mennonites Sandy and Jerry Tucker, the Galilean Home Ministries is a permanent home for some in need of constant care. It also offers temporary refuge for others like Hondurans Dina, who is recovering from hand and foot surgery, and Frankie who underwent a leg amputation.

Photo by Pat McDonogh

Reason To Believe

Galilean Home Ministries residents Nathan Cochran (top) and Frankie Sierra say their bed-time prayers. Nathan is part of the organization's Angel House program, which offers care for chil-dren whose mothers are incarcerated. Frankie is recuperating from a leg amputation before re-turning to his native Honduras.

Photos by Pat McDonogh

LIBERTY

In the Angel House playroom, Kristina Foster en-tertains Anastasia McFarland whose mother is incarcerated. Like the Galilean Home Ministries founders, Foster is a volunteer.

DANVILLE

Known as the "rapper priest," Father Norman Fischer of St. Joseph's Catholic Church entertains seventh-graders at a weekend leadership retreat. Father Norman was the first African American ordained in the Lexington diocese.

Photos by James H. Kenney,
Western Kentucky University

DANVILLE

Father Norman takes blindfolded Robbie Walters on a walk through the woods at the Cliffview Retreat Center. The "trust walk" is designed to teach interdependence. "We need to help people," says Father Norman. "But there are also times that we need to let others help us."

DANVILLE

Cheered on by her friends and Father Norman, Connor Twyman charges across the field during a game of Red Rover to break the line of the opposing team. Connor says the retreat was a bonding experience and helped prepare her and the other seventh-graders for their final year at Christ the King (K–8) school.

Shlomie Litvin bows to God in prayer at Anshei Sfard synagogue. His hat and formal attire are a sign of respect.

Photos by David R. Lutman

Fred Reininger wears *tefillen*, or phylacteries, around his arm and head during prayers to symbolize giving his actions, thoughts, and emotions to God. Anshei Sfard is the only orthodox synagogue in Kentucky.

Men and women are separated by partitions during prayer so they may focus on God. Iana Mosiovznik doesn't travel far to attend services; she lives next door to the synagogue.

NEW HAVEN

Trappist monks have been in Kentucky since 1848 when the Abbey of Gethsemani was founded. Brother Raphael Prendergast's day starts at 3 a.m. "I heard of a place like this when I was a little boy, where men got up in the middle of the night to pray," he says.

Photos by David R. Lutman

NEW HAVEN

The monks at Abbey of Gethsemani have made an income from their culinary labors since the 1940s, when they first made cheese. They've branched out since and now produce fudge and fruitcake as well as Port du Salut cheese. In the fudge department, Brother Frank Gerzynski readies bourbon fudge for wrapping and shipping.

SOUTH UNION
Novice Edward Olson, a member of the Fathers of Mercy, touches the cross before entering the community's common area. The evangelistic missionary order, founded in 1808, conducts retreats throughout North America to help Catholics recommit to Christ, the Holy Sacraments, and the Church.
Photos by James H. Kenney,
Western Kentucky University

SOUTH UNION

After mass, Brother William Bellrose plays ball with Joseph and Hailey McGinnis and Hollie Vincent. Brother Bill is one of 26 priests, brothers, and novices living on the 40-acre property of the Fathers of Mercy order. He is scheduled to take his final vows for the priesthood in 2005.

Parishioners at Tri-Cities Pentecostal Church lay hands on three teenagers who asked to be saved during a Wednesday night service.
Photo by Chad Allen Stevens,
Western Kentucky University

DANVILLE

Pastor Eddie Johnson delivers his weekly sermon in sign language to his 50 congregants. "We use our eyes to hear God's words," says Johnson, who is deaf and has served the Danville Deaf Baptist Mission for the past five years. It is one of 200 deaf churches in America.

Photo by James H. Kenney,
Western Kentucky University

SOUTH UNION

The Fathers of Mercy order offers Mass seven days a week at its chapel. On Sundays, 100 people from surrounding communities attend. Some wear rosaries as talismans; others keep them in constant motion, conducting their silent prayers.

Photo by James H. Kenney,
Western Kentucky University

CRESCENT SPRINGS

Sister Esther O'Hara, O.S.B., had to give up puppeteering when she got arthritis, but she still uses props—a penguin, a mouse, a little girl, an old lady, and a witch—to bring out the lessons in the stories she tells schoolkids. "They love the witch," she says.

Photos by Patrick Reddy, Cincinnati Enquirer

CRESCENT SPRINGS

The kids pay attention when Sister Esther comes to St. Joseph Elementary School. Nick Lornemann says his favorite part is when the witch tells them to eat all the candy before their parents get it.

LOUISVILLE

Ensconced on the bank of the Ohio River, the Patriots Peace Memorial honors military women and men who have died in peacetime. When a service member is killed, a glass brick inscribed with their name is set into the wall. The lantern-like design by architect David Quillen uses light to project the names to viewers inside.

Photo by Sam Upshaw, Jr.

MAPLE MOUNT

At the Ursuline Sisters of Mount Saint Joseph Convent, Sister Agnes Catherine Williams, 98, helps Sister Charles Asa Williams, 100, with her glasses. The biological sisters entered the nunnery in 1925 and 1919, respectively, and each spent more than 55 years teaching at Catholic schools in Kentucky.

Photo by L. B. Greene

HENDERSON

A week before Memorial Day, American Legion Worsham Post 40 erects crosses in Central Park for deceased veterans. "You should see the families' faces when they find the names," says Jim Hanley, who put up 2,800 crosses. "It makes it all worthwhile." Hannah Payne's parents look for her grandfather's name.

Photo by Tim Broekema, Western Kentucky University

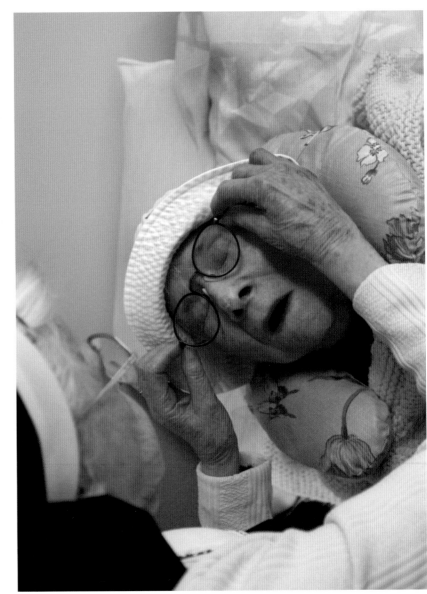

RUSSELL SPRINGS

"'I'm trying to take as many people to heaven with me as I can,'" says evangelist Dewey Cooper about the 35 multidirectional signs he has erected all over southern Kentucky. The 81-year-old digs the holes, puts up the 4x4s, and attaches the painted placards.

Photo by James H. Kenney,
Western Kentucky University

CUMBERLAND

The path to salvation is illuminated with fluorescent lights at this Pentecostal church.

Photo by Chad Allen Stevens,
Western Kentucky University

SALYERSVILLE
A Magoffin County pickup truck announces its
allegiances to God and country.
Photo by John Isaac

LOUISVILLE
David Newton watches the *American Queen* dock at Cox Park after its weeklong Ohio River excursion between Pittsburgh and Louisville. Built in 1995 and modeled after 19th-century steamboats, the ship gives 436 passengers a taste of the river-cruising days of yore.
Photo by Pat McDonogh

Our Town

HENDERSON

Released from the Army in 1945, Edward "Smitty" Smith returned to Kentucky to marry his sweetheart Juanita and earn his barber's license. He worked in hotels and, in 1973, opened his own shop. Despite the loss of both kidneys (and enduring dialysis three times a week), Smitty keeps his business—and his life—going. "I love talking to the customers," he says.

Photo by Denny Simmons

GLASGOW

After one too many bad haircuts, Jewell Rigdon knew a good thing when she found hairdresser Sue Frazier more than 20 years ago. Ever since, Rigdon has had her hair shampooed and set by Frazier every Friday at the Pink Carousel where Glasgow residents gather to share the latest gossip. "You hear a lot of wild stories," says Rigdon.

Photo by Bill Luster, The Courier-Journal

CAVE CITY

A 35-foot creature looms over Dinosaur World, off I-65 in south central Kentucky. Opened in 2003, the roadside attraction corralled 100 fiberglass models of the ancient reptiles, including the styrachosaurus, maiasaura, and tsintaosaurus.

Photo by Bill Luster, The Courier-Journal

CAVE CITY

In the 1930s, entrepreneurs tapped into the public's love of the Wild West by opening tepee-shaped motels, restaurants, gas stations, and gift shops along America's highways. The first two Wigwam Village motels opened in Kentucky in 1937. The 14-unit complex on Highway 31 outside Cave City—one of the originals—continues to draw overnight visitors.

Photo by Patrick L. Pfister, pfoto.com

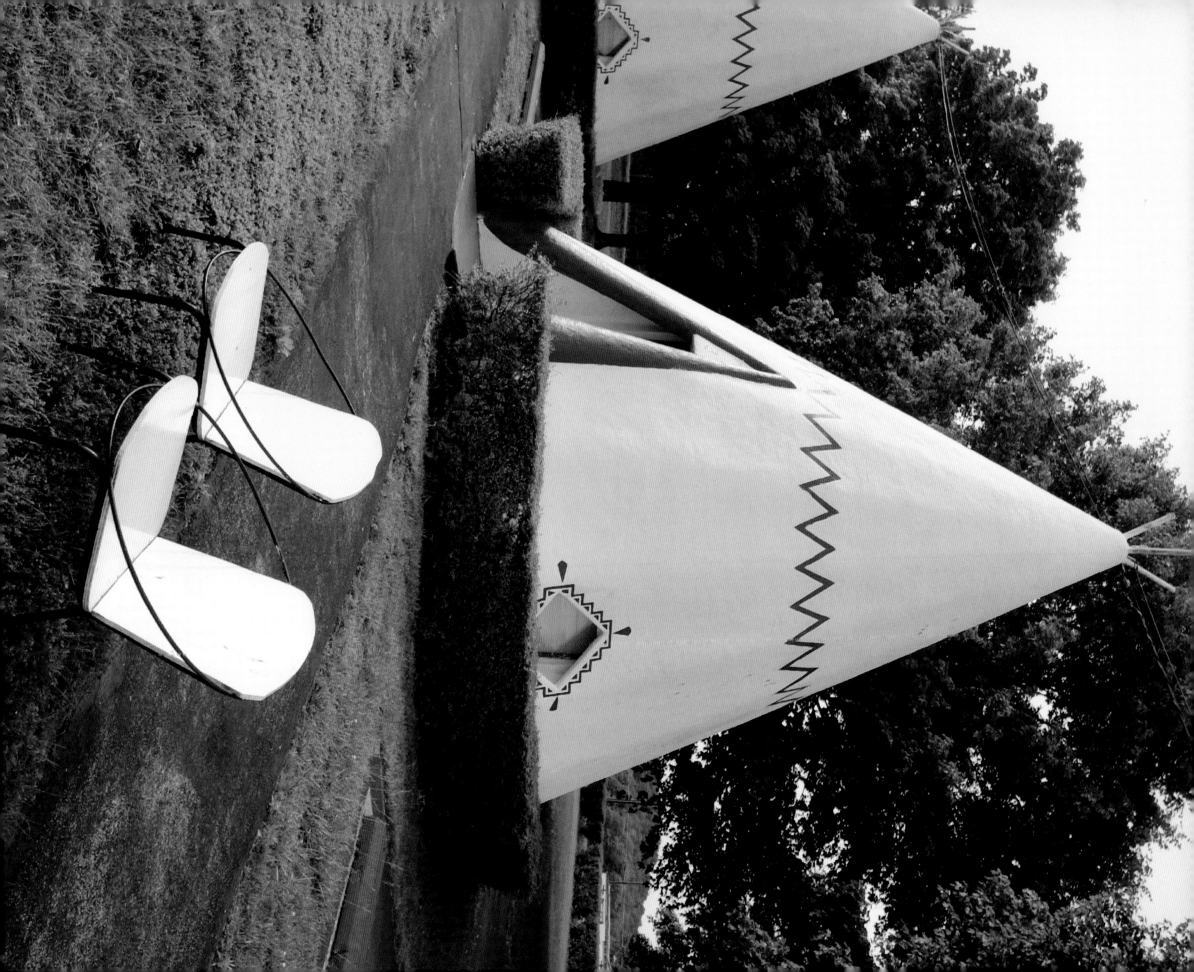

LOUISVILLE

With the Big Four Bridge in the background, the smokestacks of the *Belle of Louisville* riverboat frame the twilight. Built in Pittsburgh in 1914 as the *Idlewild*, the 800-person paddlewheeler is one of only six excursion steamers still plying the rivers of America.
Photo by Pat McDonogh

COVINGTON

Constructed during the Civil War, the 1,056-foot Roebling Suspension Bridge was a protoype for engineer John A. Roebling's later and larger Brooklyn Bridge, begun in 1869. The first bridge across the Ohio River linking Cincinnati and northern Kentucky, the "Cincinnati Bridge" replaced thousands of daily ferry crossings.
Photo by Scott R. Raper

LEXINGTON

PhD candidate Chris Green climbs the stairwell at the University of Kentucky's William T. Young Library. Opened in 1998, the library houses 1.2 million books, 50 miles of fiber-optic cable, 3,600 network ports, and 600 computers for researchers and staff.
Photo by Charles Bertram

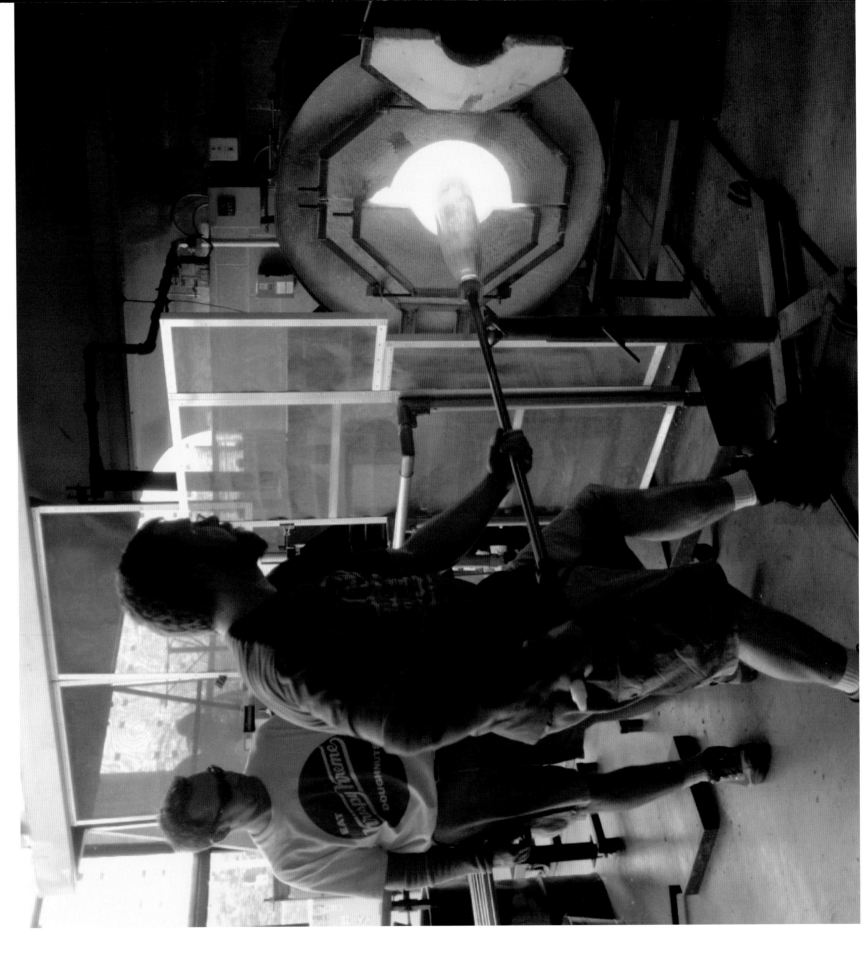

LOUISVILLE

At the Glassworks hotshop, Paul Nelson (left) and Matt Nay (right) help John Miller (center) fire up his *Blue Plate Special*, to consist of a super-sized hamburger, fries, and 3-foot-tall ketchup bottle. Opened in 2001, the nonprofit center offers artists three studios and two galleries where they can work and display their crafts.
Photo by Victor Allen Simon

LOUISVILLE

Like flowers, Louisville artist Greg Fleischaker's two-tone vases bloom from the shelves at Glassworks Gallery.

Photo by Pat McDonogh

LOUISVILLE

"Frit," or ground colored glass, is mixed in with clear, molten glass during the blowing process to give radiant color to the finished project.

Photo by Pat McDonogh

LEXINGTON

Music, food and mini trucks are all part of the fun at the annual Shriners Hospital Parade. The minis, a Shriners tradition, replicate standard cars, race cars, and big rigs. Most of the diminutive vehicles are built around the frames of golf carts and range in price from $1,600 to $6,500.

Photo by Janet Worne, Lexington Herald-Leader

LOUISVILLE

Scenes from a wedding: At a River Valley Club wedding reception, beaded fishnet draws a photographer's attention.

Photo by Dan Dry

CORYDON

Kentucky native Odie Lee Brooks is partial to her porch. She likes watching neighbors go by, swinging on the bench seat with her two grandchildren, and playing with her six cats.

Photo by Denny Simmons

PADUCAH

Yo Yo Club members Pat Lewis, Carolyn Carver, Charlotte Roberts, Anita Manning, and Virginia Hancock work on a charity quilt in the lobby of the museum of the American Quilter's Society. The women donate their quilts to the local homeless shelter and pregnancy crisis center, as well as to fundraising auctions.

Photo by Jim Roshan, jimroshan.com

LOUISVILLE

Viewers at the University of Louisville's Ekstrom Library examine photographer Bill Luster's retrospective, "Frames from the Heart." Luster, a staff photographer at the *Louisville Courier-Journal* and freelance photographer for the National Geographic Society, is also featured in *Kentucky 24/7*.

Photo by Marcy Nighswander

AUBURN

At the annual Logan County Bluegrass Jam, Sydni Perry, 10, bows her fiddle with fellow musicians. For the past year, she has been singing and playing fiddle in her parents' band, Temperance Road. Sydni also sings lead and harmonies on their CDs "Daddy's D-35" and "Three Generations Chasing a Dream."

***Photo by Jeanie Adams-Smith,
Western Kentucky University***

SALYERSVILLE

When he's not producing his gospel music TV show, selling salvage to benefit a soup kitchen, or building houses for the poor, Preacher Doc Holliday (white shirt) jams with local bluegrass musicians. Here, in front of the salvage shop, the 70-year-old croons to the improvisations of Clyde Marshall, Adam Collinsworth, Michael Gibson, and Mike Cole.

Photo by John Isaac

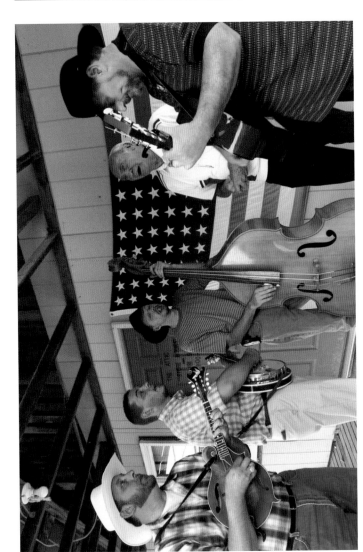

LOUISVILLE

Jose Vergara and wife Marcela Gongora execute a spin *con sabor* at Club Salsa. The couple moved from Mexico City in 2002 when Vergara, a sales manager for an international electronic components company, was transferred to Louisville. Latinos, the nation's largest minority group, number 60,000 in Kentucky.

Photo by Pat McDonogh

RED RIVER GORGE

Evening fog rises after a day of thunder-storms in eastern Kentucky. Part of the Daniel Boone National Forest, the rugged and protected terrain of the Red River Gorge is carpeted with hickory, walnut, elm, ash, maple, and pine.

Photo by David Coyle

CAVE RUN LAKE

East of Lexington, Cave Run Lake covers 8,270 acres in the Daniel Boone National Forest. A popular recreation area, the lake was created in 1974 by damming the Licking River to control flooding downstream.

Photo by Ron Garrison

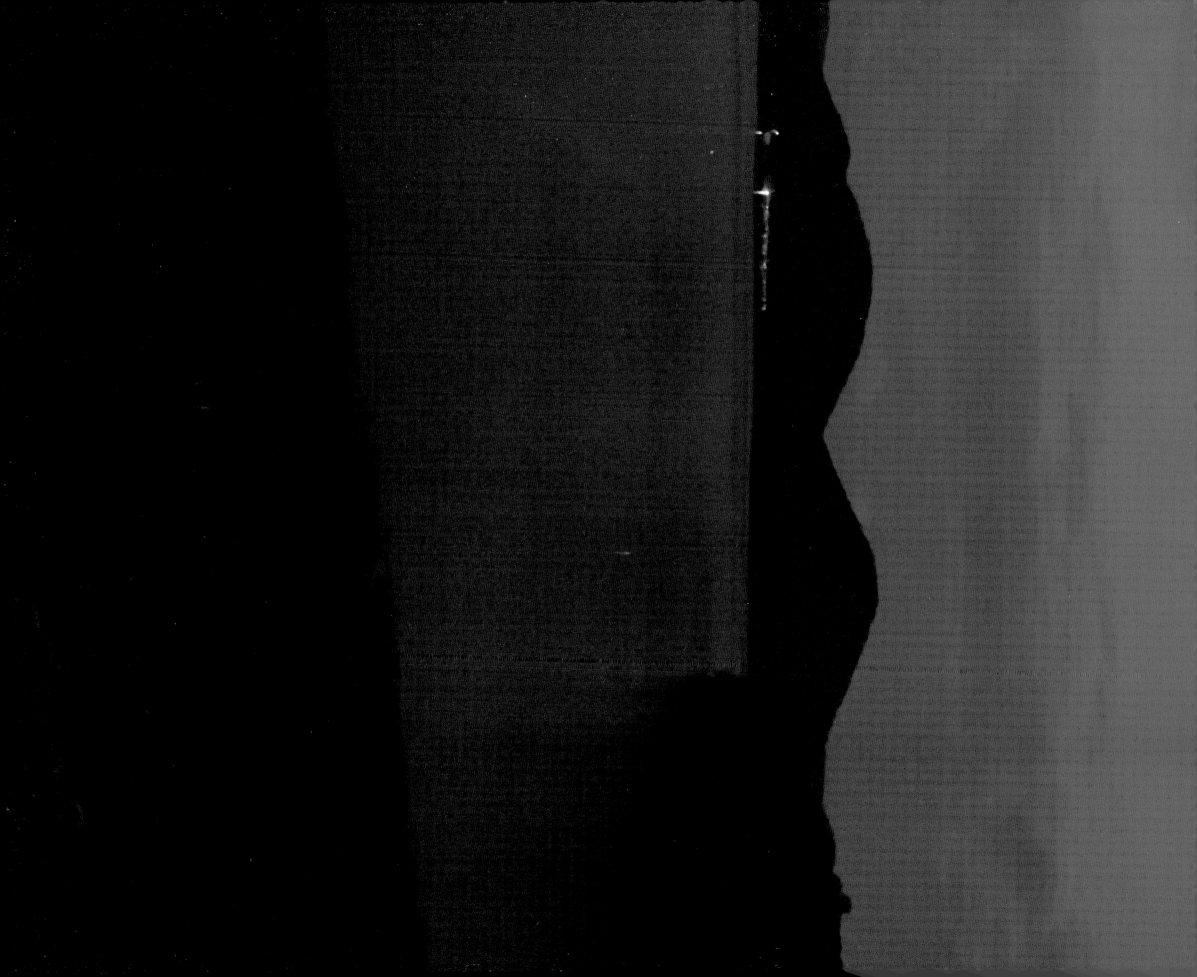

SHOOT

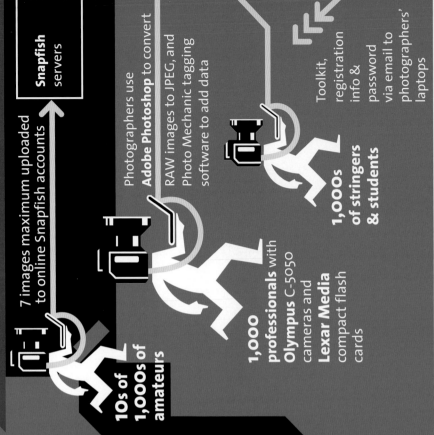

Snapfish servers

7 images maximum uploaded to online Snapfish accounts

10s of 1,000s of amateurs

Photographers use **Adobe Photoshop** to convert RAW images to JPEG, and Photo Mechanic tagging software to add data

1,000 professionals with **Olympus** C-5050 cameras and **Lexar Media** compact flash cards

Toolkit, registration info & password via email to photographers' laptops

1,000s of stringers & students

DESIGN & PUBLISH

InDesign layouts output via **Acrobat** to PDF format

Printer

5 graphic design and production teams

50 state posters designed by 50 AIGA member firms

51 books: one national, 50 states

Produced by 24/7 Media, published by DK Publishing

The week of May 12-18, 2003, more than 25,000 professional and amateur photographers spread out across the nation to shoot over a million digital photographs with the goal of capturing the essence of daily life in America.

The professional photographers were equipped with Adobe Photoshop and Adobe Album software, Olympus C-5050 digital cameras, and Lexar Media's high-speed compact flash cards.

The 1,000 professional contract photographers plus another 5,000 stringers and students sent their images via FTP (file transfer protocol) directly to the *America 24/7* website. Meanwhile, thousands of amateur photographers uploaded their images to Snapfish's servers.

At *America 24/7*'s Mission Control headquarters, located at CNET in San Francisco, dozens of picture editors from the nation's most prestigious publications culled the images down to 25,000 of the very best, using Photo Mechanic by Camera Bits. These photos were transferred into Webware's ActiveMedia Digital Asset Management (DAM) system, which served as a central image library and enabled the designers to track, search, distribute, and reformat the images for the creation of the 51 books, foreign language editions, web and magazine syndication, posters, and exhibitions.

Once in the DAM, images were optimized (and in some cases resampled to increase image resolution) using Adobe Photoshop. Adobe InDesign and Adobe InCopy were used to design and produce the 51 books, which were edited and reviewed in multiple locations around the world in the form of Adobe Acrobat PDFs. Epson Stylus printers were used for photo proofing and to produce large-format images for exhibitions. The companies providing support for the *America 24/7* project offer many of the essential components for anyone building a digital darkroom. We encourage you to read more on the following pages about their respective roles in making *America 24/7* possible.

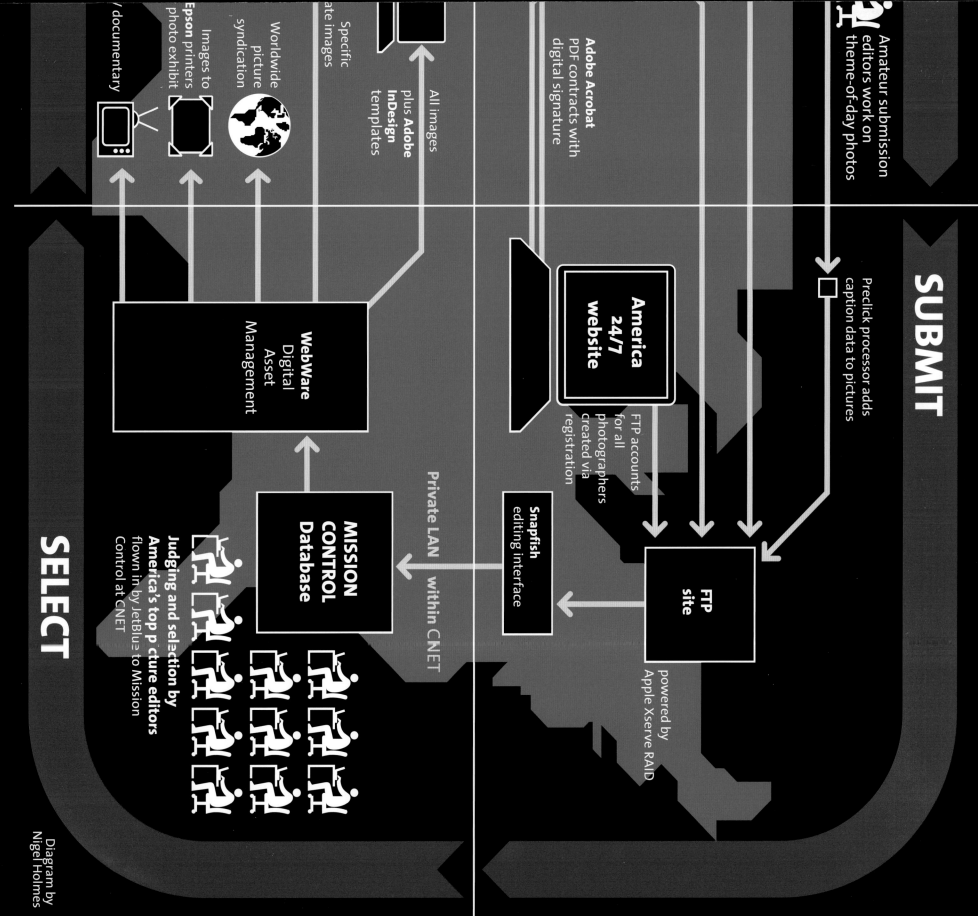

SUBMIT

Amateur submission editors work on theme-of-day photos

Preclick processor adds caption data to pictures

Adobe Acrobat
PDF contracts with digital signature

America 24/7 website

FTP accounts for all photographers created via registration

FTP site

powered by Apple Xserve RAID

All images

plus **Adobe InDesign** templates

Specific ate images

WebWare
Digital Asset Management

Worldwide picture syndication

Images to **Epson** printers photo exhibit

documentary

Private LAN within CNET

Snapfish editing interface

MISSION CONTROL Database

Judging and selection by America's top picture editors
flown in by JetBlue to Mission Control at CNET

SELECT

Diagram by
Nigel Holmes

About Our Sponsors

Adobe

America 24/7 gave digital photographers of all levels the opportunity to share their visions of what it means to live in the United States. This project was made possible by a digital photography revolution that is dramatically changing and improving picture-taking for professionals and amateurs alike. And an Adobe product, Photoshop®, has been at the center of this sea change.

Adobe's products reflect our customers' passion for the creative process, be it the photographer, graphic designer, layout artist, or printer. Adobe is the Publishing and Imaging Software Partner for *America 24/7* and products such as Adobe InDesign®, Photoshop, Acrobat®, and Illustrator® were used to produce this stunning book in a matter of weeks. We hope that our software has helped do justice to the mythic images, contributed by well-known photographers and the inspired hobbyist.

Adobe is proud to be a lead sponsor of *America 24/7*, a project that celebrates the vibrancy of the American spirit: the same spirit that helped found Adobe and inspires our employees and customers to deliver the very best.

Bruce Chizen
President and CEO
Adobe Systems Incorporated

OLYMPUS

Olympus, a global technology leader in designing precision healthcare solutions and innovative consumer electronics, is proud to be the official digital camera sponsor of *America 24/7*. The opportunity to introduce Americans from coast to coast to the thrill, excitement, and possibility of digital photography makes the vision behind this book a perfect fit for Olympus, a leader in digital cameras since 1996.

For most people, the essence of digital photography is best grasped through firsthand experience with the technology, which is precisely what *America 24/7* is about. We understand that direct experience is the pathway to inspiration, and welcome opportunities like this sponsorship to bring the power of the digital experience into the lives of people everywhere. To Olympus, *America 24/7* offers a platform to help realize a core mission: to deliver and make accessible the power of the digital experience to millions of American photographers, amateurs, and professionals alike.

The 1,000 professional photographers contracted to shoot on the *America 24/7* project were all equipped with Olympus C-5050 digital cameras. Like all Olympus products, the C-5050 is offered by a company well known for designing, manufacturing, and servicing products used by professionals to perform their work, every day. Olympus is a customer-centric company committed to working one-to-one with a diverse group of professionals. From biomedical researchers who use our clinical microscopes, to doctors who perform life-saving procedures with our endoscopes, to professional photographers who use cameras in their daily work, Olympus is a trusted brand.

The digital imaging technology involved with *America 24/7* has enabled the soul of America to be visually conveyed, not just by professional observers, but by the American public who participated in this project—the very people who collectively breath life into this country's existence each day.

We are proud to be enabling so many photographers to capture the pictures on these pages that tell the story of who we are as a nation. From sea to shining sea, digital imagery allows us to connect to one another in ways we never dreamed possible.

At Olympus, our ideas have proliferated as rapidly as technology has evolved. We have channeled these visions into breakthrough products and solutions to meet the demands of our changing world-products like microscopes, endoscopes, and digital voice recorders, supported by the highly regarded training, educational, and consulting services we offer our customers.

Today, 83 years after we introduced our first microscope, we remain as young, as curious, and as committed as ever.

LEXAR Media

Lexar Media has grown from the digital photography revolution, which is why we are proud to have supplied the digital memory cards used in the America 24/7 project. Lexar Media's high-performance memory cards utilize our unique and patented controller coupled with high-speed flash memory from Samsung, the world's largest flash memory supplier. This powerful combination brings out the ultimate performance of any digital camera.

Photographers who demand the most from their equipment choose our products for their advanced features like write speeds up to 40X, Write Acceleration technology for enabled cameras, and Image Rescue, which recovers previously deleted or lost images. Leading camera manufacturers bundle Lexar Media digital memory cards with their cameras because they value its performance and reliability.

Lexar Media is at the forefront of digital photography as it transforms picture-taking worldwide, and we will continue to be a leader with new and innovative solutions for professionals and amateurs alike.

Snapfish, which developed the technology behind the *America 24/7* amateur photo event, is a leading online photo service, with more than 5 million members and 100 million photos posted online. Snapfish enables both film and digital camera owners to share, print, and store their most important photo memories, at prices that cannot be equaled. Digital camera users upload photos into a password-protected online album for free. Users can also order film-quality prints on professional photographic paper for as low as 25¢. Film camera users get a full set of prints, plus online sharing and storage, for just $2.99 per roll.

JetBlue Airways is proud to be *America 24/7's* preferred carrier, flying photographers, photo editors, and organizers across the United States.

Winner of Condé Nast Traveler's *Readers' Choice Awards for Best Domestic Airline 2002*, JetBlue provides friendly service and low fares for travelers in 22 cities in nine states across America.

On behalf of JetBlue's 5,000 crew members, we're excited to be involved in this remarkable project, and for the opportunity to serve American travelers each and every day, coast to coast, 24/7.

WebWare Corporation is pleased to be a major sponsor of the *America 24/7* project. We take pride in being part of a groundbreaking adventure that is stretching the boundaries—and the right answer from an ocean of imagination—in digital photography, digital asset management, publishing, news, and global events.

Our ActiveMedia Enterprise™ digital asset management software is the "nerve center" of *America 24/7*, the central repository for managing, sharing, and collaborating on the project's photographs. From photo editors and book publishers to 24/7's media relations and marketing personnel, ActiveMedia provides the application support that links all facets of the project team to the content worldwide.

WebWare helps Global 2000 firms securely manage, reuse, and distribute media assets locally or globally. Its suite of ActiveMedia software products provide powerful media services platforms for integrating rich media into content management systems marketing and communication portals; web publishing systems; and e-commerce portals.

Special thanks to additional contributors: FileMaker, Apple, Camera Bits, LaCie, Now Software, Preclick, Outpost Digital, Xerox, Microsoft, WoodWing Software, net-linx Publishing Solutions, and Radical Media. The Savoy Hotel, San Francisco; The Pan Pacific, San Francisco; Four Seasons Hotel, San Francisco; and The Queen Anne Hotel. Photography editing facilities were generously hosted by CNET Networks, Inc.

Google's mission is to organize the world's information and make it universally accessible and useful.

With our focus on plucking just the right answer from an ocean of data, we were naturally drawn to the *America 24/7* project. The book you hold is a compendium of images of American life distilled from thousands of photographs and infinite possibilities. Are you looking for emotion? Narrative? Shadows? Light? It's all here, thanks to a multitude of photographers and writers creating links between you, the reader, and a sea of wonderful stories. We celebrate the connections that constitute the human experience and are pleased to help engender them. And we're pleased to have been a small part of this project, which captures the results of that interaction so vividly, so dynamically, and so dramatically.

Founded in 1995, eBay created a powerful platform for the sale of goods and services by a passionate community of individuals and businesses. On any given day, there are millions of items across thousands of categories for sale on eBay. eBay enables trade on a local, national and international basis with customized sites in markets around the world.

Through an array of services, such as its payment solution provider PayPal, eBay is enabling global e-commerce for an ever-growing online community.

Digital Pond has been a leading creator of large graphic displays for museums, corporations, trade shows, retail environments and fine art since 1992.

We were proud to bring together our creative, print and display capabilities to produce signage and displays for mission control, critical retouching for numerous key images for the book, and art galleries for the New York Public Library and Bryant Park.

The Pond's team and SplashPic® Online service enabled us to nimbly design, produce and install over 200 large graphic panels in two NYC locations within the truly "24/7" production schedule of less than ten days.

Participating Photographers

Coordinator: Bill Luster,* Senior Enterprise Photographer, Associate Photo Editor, *The Courier-Journal*

Jeanie Adams-Smith, Western Kentucky University
Charles Bertram
Tim Broekema*, Western Kentucky University
David Coyle
Dan Dry
Douglas Ettin
Kenneth Gantz
Ron Garrison
L. B. Greene
John Isaac
James H. Kenney, Western Kentucky University
Michael Leitz
Bill Luster*, *The Courier-Journal*
David R. Lutman
Pat McDonogh*
David Nash
Marcy Nighswander

Jeff Osborne
Patrick L. Pfister, pfoto.com
Katie Ralph
Scott R. Raper
Patrick Reddy, *Cincinnati Enquirer*
David Robertson
Jim Roshan, jimroshan.com
Denny Simmons
Victor Allen Simon
Pam Spaulding
David Stephenson
Chad Allen Stevens, Western Kentucky University
Michael Tucker
Sam Upshaw, Jr.
Ken Weaver
Janet Worne, *Lexington Herald-Leader*

*Pulitzer Prize winner

Thumbnail Picture Credits

Credits for thumbnail photographs are listed by the page number and are in order from left to right.

20 Patrick L. Pfister, pfoto.com
Pat McDonogh
David Stephenson
Jeanie Adams-Smith, Western Kentucky University
Dan Dry
David Stephenson
David Stephenson

21 Dan Dry
Weasie Gaines
Dan Dry
David Stephenson
Jeanie Adams-Smith, Western Kentucky University
Tim Girton
Sam Upshaw, Jr.

22 Dan Dry
Charles Bertram
Dan Dry
Tim Girton
Chad Allen Stevens, Western Kentucky University
Weasie Gaines
Weasie Gaines

23 Dan Brandenburg
Dan Dry
Ron Garrison
Chad Allen Stevens, Western Kentucky University
Tim Girton
Dan Dry
Tim Girton

24 Jeanie Adams-Smith, Western Kentucky University
John Isaac
Jeanie Adams-Smith, Western Kentucky University
Jeanie Adams-Smith, Western Kentucky University
Patrick Reddy, *Cincinnati Enquirer*
Jeanie Adams-Smith, Western Kentucky University
Jeanie Adams-Smith, Western Kentucky University

25 Jeanie Adams-Smith, Western Kentucky University
Jeanie Adams-Smith, Western Kentucky University
Jeanie Adams-Smith, Western Kentucky University
Jeanie Adams-Smith, Western Kentucky University
Jeanie Adams-Smith, Western Kentucky University
John Isaac
Jeanie Adams-Smith, Western Kentucky University

26 David R. Lutman
David R. Lutman
Tim Broekema, Western Kentucky University
David R. Lutman
David R. Lutman
David R. Lutman
David R. Lutman

27 David R. Lutman
David R. Lutman
David R. Lutman
Tim Broekema, Western Kentucky University
David R. Lutman
Tim Broekema, Western Kentucky University
David R. Lutman

28 Dan Dry
Chad Allen Stevens, Western Kentucky University
Weasie Gaines
Chad Allen Stevens, Western Kentucky University
Patrick Reddy, *Cincinnati Enquirer*
Chad Allen Stevens, Western Kentucky University
Patrick Reddy, *Cincinnati Enquirer*

29 Chad Allen Stevens, Western Kentucky University
C. Thomas Hardin
Dan Dry
Dan Dry
Weasie Gaines
Dan Dry
Patrick Reddy, *Cincinnati Enquirer*

32 James H. Kenney, Western Kentucky University
Jeanie Adams-Smith, Western Kentucky University
James H. Kenney, Western Kentucky University
James H. Kenney, Western Kentucky University
John Isaac
James H. Kenney, Western Kentucky University
Tim Girton

33 James H. Kenney, Western Kentucky University
James H. Kenney, Western Kentucky University
James H. Kenney, Western Kentucky University
James H. Kenney, Western Kentucky University
James H. Kenney, Western Kentucky University
L. B. Greene
Ron Garrison

34 John Isaac
Jeanie Adams-Smith, Western Kentucky University
Jeanie Adams-Smith, Western Kentucky University
Jeanie Adams-Smith, Western Kentucky University
Jeanie Adams-Smith, Western Kentucky University
Ron Garrison
Jeanie Adams-Smith, Western Kentucky University

36 Bill Luster, The Courier-Journal
James H. Kenney, Western Kentucky University
Bill Luster, *The Courier-Journal*
David Stephenson
Bill Luster, *The Courier-Journal*
Bill Luster, *The Courier-Journal*
Janet Worne, *Lexington Herald-Leader*

37 Janet Worne, *Lexington Herald-Leader*
David Stephenson
James H. Kenney, Western Kentucky University
Bill Luster, *The Courier-Journal*
Bill Luster, *The Courier-Journal*
Janet Worne, *Lexington Herald-Leader*
James H. Kenney, Western Kentucky University

38 Bill Luster, *The Courier-Journal*
Chad Allen Stevens, Western Kentucky University
Bill Luster, *The Courier-Journal*
Bill Luster, *The Courier-Journal*
Bill Luster, *The Courier-Journal*
Bill Luster, *The Courier-Journal*

39 David Stephenson
Pam Spaulding
Bill Luster, *The Courier-Journal*
Janet Worne, *Lexington Herald-Leader*
Bill Luster, *The Courier-Journal*
Dan Dry
John Isaac

40 David Stephenson
Charles Bertram
Chad Allen Stevens, Western Kentucky University
Chad Allen Stevens, Western Kentucky University
Ken Weaver
Chad Allen Stevens, Western Kentucky University
John Isaac

41 Charles Bertram
John Isaac
David Stephenson
Charles Bertram
Pat McDonogh
Pam Spaulding
Chad Allen Stevens, Western Kentucky University

50 Chad Allen Stevens, Western Kentucky University
Bill Luster, *The Courier-Journal*
Chad Allen Stevens, Western Kentucky University
Bill Luster, *The Courier-Journal*
Dan Dry
Bill Luster, *The Courier-Journal*

51 Chad Allen Stevens, Western Kentucky University
Bill Luster, *The Courier-Journal*
Dan Dry
Chad Allen Stevens, Western Kentucky University
Dan Dry
Dan Dry

52 Bill Luster, *The Courier-Journal*
Bill Luster, *The Courier-Journal*
Bill Luster, *The Courier-Journal*
Bill Luster, *The Courier-Journal*
Bill Luster, *The Courier-Journal*
Bill Luster, *The Courier-Journal*
Bill Luster, *The Courier-Journal*

53 Bill Luster, *The Courier-Journal*
Bill Luster, *The Courier-Journal*
Bill Luster, *The Courier-Journal*
Bill Luster, *The Courier-Journal*
Bill Luster, *The Courier-Journal*
Bill Luster, *The Courier-Journal*
Bill Luster, *The Courier-Journal*

56 David Stephenson
John Russell, Maximum Exposure
Weasie Gaines
David Stephenson
Pam Spaulding
Pam Spaulding

57 Janet Worne, *Lexington Herald-Leader*
Charles Bertram
Pam Spaulding
David Stephenson
Charles Bertram
Janet Worne, *Lexington Herald-Leader*
Pam Spaulding

58 Charles Bertram
Charles Bertram
Charles Bertram
Ken Weaver
David Stephenson
Ken Weaver
Charles Bertram

59 David Stephenson
Charles Bertram
John Isaac
Ken Weaver
Charles Bertram
Ken Weaver
Charles Bertram

60 Ken Weaver
Ron Garrison
Ken Weaver
Ron Garrison
Ron Garrison
Ron Garrison
Ken Weaver

61 Ken Weaver
Ron Garrison
Ken Weaver
Ron Garrison
Ron Garrison
Ken Weaver
Ron Garrison

62 Victor Allen Simon
Tim Girton
Pat McDonogh
Chad Allen Stevens, Western Kentucky University
Chad Allen Stevens, Western Kentucky University
Dan Brandenburg
Pat McDonogh

63 Dan Dry
Pat McDonogh
Dan Dry
Pat McDonogh
Pat McDonogh
Pat McDonogh
Tim Girton

64 Janet Worne, *Lexington Herald-Leader*
James H. Kenney, Western Kentucky University
Janet Worne, *Lexington Herald-Leader*
James H. Kenney, Western Kentucky University
James H. Kenney, Western Kentucky University
Janet Worne, *Lexington Herald-Leader*
James H. Kenney, Western Kentucky University

65 James H. Kenney, Western Kentucky University
James H. Kenney, Western Kentucky University
Janet Worne, *Lexington Herald-Leader*
James H. Kenney, Western Kentucky University
Janet Worne, *Lexington Herald-Leader*
Janet Worne, *Lexington Herald-Leader*

66 Jeanie Adams-Smith, Western Kentucky University
David Stephenson
Dan Dry
Dan Brandenburg
Jeanie Adams-Smith, Western Kentucky University
Jeanie Adams-Smith, Western Kentucky University
Dan Brandenburg

67 Sam Upshaw, Jr.
Charles Bertram
Charles Bertram
Jeanie Adams-Smith, Western Kentucky University
Charles Bertram
David R. Lutman
David Stephenson

69 Pat McDonogh
Pat McDonogh
Pat McDonogh
Pat McDonogh
Pat McDonogh
Pat McDonogh

70 Dan Dry
Dan Dry
Sam Upshaw, Jr.
Dan Dry
Dan Dry
Jim Roshan, jimroshan.com
Dan Dry

71 Jim Roshan, jimroshan.com
Jim Roshan, jimroshan.com
Dan Dry
David R. Lutman
Jim Roshan, jimroshan.com
James H. Kenney, Western Kentucky University
Tim Broekema, Western Kentucky University
Ronald Hoover

72 John Isaac
John Isaac
John Isaac
John Isaac
John Isaac
John Isaac

74 Dan Dry
Jim Roshan, jimroshan.com
Dan Dry
David R. Lutman
Jim Roshan, jimroshan.com
David R. Lutman
Jim Roshan, jimroshan.com
David R. Lutman
Jim Roshan, jimroshan.com

75 David R. Lutman
David R. Lutman
Jim Roshan, jimroshan.com
David R. Lutman
Jim Roshan, jimroshan.com
Jim Roshan, jimroshan.com
Jim Roshan, jimroshan.com

76 Sam Upshaw, Jr.
Jim Roshan, jimroshan.com
Jim Roshan, jimroshan.com
Sam Upshaw, Jr.
Jim Roshan, jimroshan.com
Jim Roshan, jimroshan.com
Jim Roshan, jimroshan.com
Jim Roshan, jimroshan.com

80 Tim Girton
Chad Allen Stevens, Western Kentucky University
David R. Lutman
Ron Garrison
Jeanie Adams-Smith, Western Kentucky University
Jeanie Adams-Smith, Western Kentucky University
Ken Weaver

81 Jeanie Adams-Smith, Western Kentucky University
Ken Weaver
Ron Garrison
Ken Weaver
Pam Spaulding
Ron Garrison
David Robertson

82 James H. Kenney, Western Kentucky University
John Isaac
David Stephenson
Patrick L. Pfister, pfoto.com
Weasie Gaines
Pam Spaulding
Patrick Reddy, Cincinnati Enquirer

83 Tim Girton
Pat McDonogh
Patrick Reddy, Cincinnati Enquirer
Pam Spaulding
Tim Broekema, Western Kentucky University
Pat McDonogh
Weasie Gaines

85 David Coyle
David Coyle
David Coyle
David Coyle
David Coyle
David Coyle
David Coyle

86 Tim Girton
Ken Weaver
James H. Kenney, Western Kentucky University
Pam Spaulding
David Stephenson
Chad Allen Stevens, Western Kentucky University
John Russell, MaximumExposure

87 Chad Allen Stevens, Western Kentucky University
Ronald Hoover
Dan Dry
David R. Lutman
James H. Kenney, Western Kentucky University
Tim Broekema, Western Kentucky University
Ronald Hoover

88 Chad Allen Stevens, Western Kentucky University
Charles Bertram
Dan Dry
Charles Bertram
Charles Bertram
Chad Allen Stevens, Western Kentucky University
Charles Bertram

89 Chad Allen Stevens, Western Kentucky University
Tim Broekema, Western Kentucky University
David Stephenson
Ken Weaver
Ken Weaver
Ken Weaver
Tim Broekema, Western Kentucky University

90 Ken Weaver
Charles Bertram
Ken Weaver
Chad Allen Stevens, Western Kentucky University
Dan Brandenburg
Ken Weaver
Janet Worne, Lexington Herald-Leader

91 Dan Brandenburg
Ken Weaver
Ken Weaver
Ken Weaver
Ken Weaver
Ken Weaver

94 Bill Luster, The Courier Journal
David Stephenson
Dan Dry
Jeanie Adams-Smith, Western Kentucky University
John Isaac
David Stephenson

95 Patrick L. Pfister, pfoto.com
Jeanie Adams-Smith, Western Kentucky University
David Stephenson
Jeanie Adams-Smith, Western Kentucky University
Patrick L. Pfister, pfoto.com
Jeanie Adams-Smith, Western Kentucky University
Dan Dry

99 Pat McDonogh
Pat McDonogh
Pat McDonogh
Pat McDonogh
Pat McDonogh
Pat McDonogh
Pat McDonogh

100 James H. Kenney, Western Kentucky University
Chad Allen Stevens, Western Kentucky University
Charles Bertram
James H. Kenney, Western Kentucky University
James H. Kenney, Western Kentucky University
James H. Kenney, Western Kentucky University
John Isaac

101 James H. Kenney, Western Kentucky University
James H. Kenney, Western Kentucky University
James H. Kenney, Western Kentucky University
James H. Kenney, Western Kentucky University
James H. Kenney, Western Kentucky University
James H. Kenney, Western Kentucky University
Pam Spaulding

103 David R. Lutman
David R. Lutman
David R. Lutman
David R. Lutman
David R. Lutman
David R. Lutman
David R. Lutman

105 David R. Lutman
David R. Lutman
David R. Lutman
David R. Lutman
David R. Lutman
David R. Lutman
David R. Lutman

108 James H. Kenney, Western Kentucky University
Chad Allen Stevens, Western Kentucky University
James H. Kenney, Western Kentucky University
James H. Kenney, Western Kentucky University
James H. Kenney, Western Kentucky University
James H. Kenney, Western Kentucky University

109 James H. Kenney, Western Kentucky University
James H. Kenney, Western Kentucky University
Chad Allen Stevens, Western Kentucky University
James H. Kenney, Western Kentucky University
Chad Allen Stevens, Western Kentucky University
James H. Kenney, Western Kentucky University

110 Chad Allen Stevens, Western Kentucky University
Patrick Reddy, Cincinnati Enquirer
Dan Dry
Dan Dry
Janet Worne, Lexington Herald-Leader
Chad Allen Stevens, Western Kentucky University
James H. Kenney, Western Kentucky University

111 Pat McDonogh
Patrick L. Pfister, pfoto.com
Pat McDonogh
Patrick Reddy, Cincinnati Enquirer
Chad Allen Stevens, Western Kentucky University
Chad Allen Stevens, Western Kentucky University
Patrick Reddy, Cincinnati Enquirer

112 Tim Broekema, Western Kentucky University
Sam Upshaw, Jr.
Denny Simmons
L. B. Greene
Dan Dry
Tim Broekema, Western Kentucky University
L. B. Greene

114 David R. Lutman
James H. Kenney, Western Kentucky University
Chad Allen Stevens, Western Kentucky University
Dan Brandenburg
Chad Allen Stevens, Western Kentucky University
Jeanie Adams-Smith, Western Kentucky University
Charles Bertram

115 Janet Worne, Lexington Herald-Leader
Chad Allen Stevens, Western Kentucky University
Pat McDonogh
Janet Worne, Lexington Herald-Leader
John Isaac
Ron Garrison
Dan Brandenburg

118 Bill Luster, The Courier-Journal
Denny Simmons
Bill Luster, The Courier-Journal
John Isaac
Bill Luster, The Courier-Journal
Bill Luster, The Courier-Journal
Denny Simmons

119 Bill Luster, The Courier-Journal
Sam Upshaw, Jr.
Bill Luster, The Courier-Journal
Denny Simmons
Bill Luster, The Courier-Journal
Bill Luster, The Courier-Journal
Sam Upshaw, Jr.

120 Jim Roshan, jimroshan.com
Bill Luster, The Courier-Journal
David Robertson
Bill Luster, The Courier-Journal
Patrick L. Pfister, pfoto.com
Janet Worne, Lexington Herald-Leader
Patrick L. Pfister, pfoto.com

122 Pat McDonogh
Pat McDonogh
Pat McDonogh
Scott R. Raper
Pat McDonogh
Charles Bertram
Dan Dry

124 Dan Dry
Charles Bertram
Chad Allen Stevens, Western Kentucky University
Pat McDonogh
Victor Allen Simon
Dan Brandenburg
Dan Dry

125 Victor Allen Simon
Pat McDonogh
Dan Dry
Patrick Reddy, Cincinnati Enquirer
Pat McDonogh
David Robertson
Patrick Reddy, Cincinnati Enquirer

127 Janet Worne, Lexington Herald-Leader
Janet Worne, Lexington Herald-Leader
Janet Worne, Lexington Herald-Leader
Dan Dry
Janet Worne, Lexington Herald-Leader
Janet Worne, Lexington Herald-Leader

128 David Robertson
Denny Simmons
David Robertson
Charles Bertram
John Isaac
Charles Bertram
Denny Simmons

129 Janet Worne, Lexington Herald-Leader
Jim Roshan, jimroshan.com
David Robertson
Sam Upshaw, Jr.
Jim Roshan, jimroshan.com
Janet Worne, Lexington Herald-Leader
John Isaac

132 Jeanie Adams-Smith, Western Kentucky University
John Isaac
Dan Dry
Jeanie Adams-Smith, Western Kentucky University
Jeanie Adams-Smith, Western Kentucky University
David Stephenson
John Isaac

133 Ron Garrison
Jeanie Adams-Smith, Western Kentucky University
Dan Dry
John Isaac
Pat McDonogh
Pam Spaulding
Chad Allen Stevens, Western Kentucky University

Staff

The *America 24/7* series was imagined years ago by our friend Oscar Dystel, a publishing legend whose vision and enthusiasm have been a source of great inspiration.

We also wish to express our gratitude to our truly visionary publisher, DK.

Rick Smolan, Project Director
David Elliot Cohen, Project Director

Administrative

Katya Able, Operations Director
Gina Privitere, Communications Director
Chuck Gathard, Technology Director
Kim Shannon, Photographer Relations Director
Erin O'Connor, Photographer Relations Intern
Leslie Hunter, Partnership Director
Annie Polk, Publicity Manager
John McAlester, Website Manager
Alex Notides, Office Manager
C. Thomas Hardin, State Photography Coordinator

Design

Brad Zucroff, Creative Director
Karen Mullarkey, Photography Director
Judy Zimola, Production Manager
David Simoni, Production Designer
Mary Dias, Production Designer
Heidi Madison, Associate Picture Editor
Don McCartney, Production Designer
Diane Dempsey Murray, Production Designer
Jan Rogers, Associate Picture Editor
Bill Shore, Production Designer and Image Artist
Larry Nighswander, Senior Picture Editor
Bill Marr, Sarah Leen, Senior Picture Editors
Peter Truskier, Workflow Consultant
Jim Birkenseer, Workflow Consultant

Editorial

Maggie Canon, Managing Editor
Curt Sanburn, Senior Editor
Teresa L. Trego, Production Editor
Lea Aschkenas, Writer
Olivia Boler, Writer
Korey Capozza, Writer
Beverly Hanly, Writer
Bridgett Novak, Writer
Alison Owings, Writer
Fred Raker, Writer
Joe Wolff, Writer
Elise O'Keefe, Copy Chief
Daisy Hernández, Copy Editor
Jennifer Wolfe, Copy Editor

Infographic Design

Nigel Holmes

Literary Agent

Carol Mann, The Carol Mann Agency

Legal Counsel

Barry Reeder, Coblentz, Patch, Duffy & Bass, LLP
Phil Feldman, Coblentz, Patch, Duffy & Bass, LLP
Gabe Perle, Ohlandt, Greeley, Ruggiero & Perle, LLP
Jon Hart, Dow, Lohnes & Albertson, PLLC
Mike Hays, Dow, Lohnes & Albertson, PLLC
Stephen Pollen, Warshaw Burstein, Cohen, Schlesinger & Kuh, LLP
Rick Pappas

Accounting and Finance

Rita Dulebohn, Accountant
Robert Powers, Calegari, Morris & Co. Accountants
Eugene Blumberg, Blumberg & Associates
Arthur Langhaus, KLS Professional Advisors Group, Inc.

Picture Editors

J. David Ake, Associated Press
Caren Alpert, formerly *Health* magazine
Simon Barnett, *Newsweek*
Caroline Couig, *San Jose Mercury News*
Mike Davis, formerly *National Geographic*
Michel duCille, *Washington Post*
Deborah Dragon, *Rolling Stone*
Victor Fisher, formerly Associated Press
Frank Folwell, *USA Today*
MaryAnne Golon, *Time*
Liz Grady, formerly *National Geographic*
Randall Greenwell, *San Francisco Chronicle*
C. Thomas Hardin, formerly *Louisville Courier-Journal*
Kathleen Hennessy, *San Francisco Chronicle*
Scot Jahn, *U.S. News & World Report*
Steve Jessmore, *Flint Journal*
John Kaplan, University of Florida
Kim Komenich, *San Francisco Chronicle*
Eliane Laffont, *Hachette Filipacchi Media*
Jean-Pierre Laffont, *Hachette Filipacchi Media*
Andrew Locke, *MSNBC*
Jose Lopez, *The New York Times*
Maria Mann, formerly AFP
Bill Marr, formerly *National Geographic*
Michele McNally, *Fortune*
James Merithew, *San Francisco Chronicle*
Eric Meskauskas, *New York Daily News*
Maddy Miller, *People* magazine
Michelle Molloy, *Newsweek*
Dolores Morrison, *New York Daily News*
Karen Mullarkey, formerly *Newsweek, Rolling Stone, Sports Illustrated*
Larry Nighswander, Ohio University School of Visual Communication
Sarah Rozen, formerly *Entertainment Weekly*
Mike Smith, *The New York Times*
Neal Ulevich, formerly Associated Press

Website and Digital Systems

Jeff Burchell, Applications Engineer

Television Documentary

Sandy Smolan, Producer/Director
Rick King, Producer/Director
Bill Medsker, Producer

Video News Release

Mike Cerre, Producer/Director

Digital Pond

Peter Hogg
Kris Knight
Roger Graham
Philip Bond
Frank De Pace
Lisa Li

Senior Advisors

Jennifer Erwitt, Strategic Advisor
Tom Walker, Creative Advisor
Megan Smith, Technology Advisor
Jon Kamen, Media and Partnership Advisor
Mark Greenberg, Partnership Advisor
Patti Richards, Publicity Advisor
Cotton Coulson, Mission Control Advisor

Executive Advisors

Sonia Land
George Craig
Carole Bidnick

Advisors

Chris Anderson
Samir Arora
Russell Brown
Craig Cline
Gayle Cline
Harlan Felt
George Fisher
Phillip Moffitt
Clement Mok
Laureen Seeger
Richard Saul Wurman

DK Publishing

Bill Barry
Joanna Bull
Therese Burke
Sarah Coltman
Christopher Davis
Todd Fries
Dick Heffernan
Jay Henry
Stuart Jackman
Stephanie Jackson
Chuck Lang
Sharon Lucas
Cathy Melnicki
Nicola Munro
Eunice Paterson
Andrew Welham

Colourscan

Jimmy Tsao
Eddie Chia
Richard Law
Josephine Yam
Paul Koh
Chee Cheng Yeong
Dan Kang

Chief Morale Officer

Goose, the dog

24/7 books available for every state. Collect the entire series of 50 books. Go to www.america24-7.com/store